Praise for Restoring Relationship

More and more therapists are finding Internal Family Systems (IFS) to be a powerful therapeutic model for helping people heal from various emotional and psychological challenges. In this book seasoned therapist Molly LaCroix demonstrates how IFS, when integrated with a Christian worldview, can enable those suffering from adversity to respond with compassion and self-awareness, rather than with shame and self-loathing, and so achieve a greater measure of emotional, psychological and spiritual wholeness. As a result, there is greater freedom to live out the Great Commandment, loving God and one another as ourselves. I highly recommend this volume for therapists, pastors and others in the Christian helping community.

  – Mark L. Strauss
    University Professor of New Testament, Bethel Seminary

Jesus told us to love one another regardless of differences and flaws. This book takes that directive seriously and provides clear steps for bringing his love not only to external others but also to the unsavory or "sinful" parts of us that the traditional church eschews. If you hate or disdain those parts, it's hard to love people who resemble them.

  – Richard C. Schwartz, PhD
    Founder of the Internal Family Systems Model

Molly LaCroix could not have more clearly laid out the case that God has equipped us with everything we need to recover from all of the pain and hurt life brings our way. Speaking from first-hand experience with the Internal Family Systems (IFS) model, the principles taught in Restoring Relationship have transformed my life. Molly brings to light the incredible ability the image of God has to cover all our fears with love, and bring about true transformation.

> – Miles McPherson
> Senior Pastor, Rock Church San Diego and author of
> *The Third Option: Hope for a Racially Divided Nation*

From exhortation to transformation, Molly LaCroix illuminates a path leading from head to heart, from pulpit to personal experiences of spiritual connection. Using insights from the Internal Family Systems approach to healing, she facilitates sacred connections on the inside that inform loving relationships on the outside. The Holy Spirit befriends and redeems every part of us; this is good news for all of us. This book is a valuable resource for anyone who wants an authentic, congruent faith.

> – Mary K. Steege, MDiv, LMFT and author of
> *The Spirit-Led Life: Christianity and the Internal Family System*

RESTORING
Relationship

RESTORING
Relationship

Transforming Fear into Love
Through Connection

Molly LaCroix, LMFT

Copyright © 2020 Molly LaCroix

ISBN: 979-8-6849-9576-7

All rights reserved.

No part of this publication may be reproduced, distributed, or transmitted in any form or by any means, including photocopying, recording, or other electronic or mechanical methods, without the prior written permission of the author, except in the case of brief quotations embodied in critical reviews and certain other noncommercial uses permitted by copyright law. For permission requests, contact the author at *mollylacroix.com*.

Unless otherwise cited, scripture quotations taken from The Holy Bible, New International Version® NIV® Copyright © 1973, 1978, 1984, 2011 by Biblica, Inc.™ Used by permission. All rights reserved worldwide.

Scripture quotations marked "The Message" are taken from THE MESSAGE, copyright © 1993, 2002, 2018 by Eugene H. Peterson. Used by permission of NavPress. All rights reserved. Represented by Tyndale House Publishers, a Division of Tyndale House Ministries.

Scripture quotations marked "TNIV" are taken from the HOLY BIBLE, TODAY'S NEW INTERNATIONAL VERSION®. Copyright © 2001, 2005 by Biblica®. Used by permission of Biblica®. All rights reserved worldwide.

Cover and interior design by Adam Thomas (*wherethewind.com*).
The image of the flower on the front cover is by grace_kat
https://www.flickr.com/photos/g_kat26/3792268494
Used under the Creative Commons Attribution-ShareAlike 2.0 Generic License:
https://creativecommons.org/licenses/by-sa/2.0/
The image was modified by removing the background, erasing a small portion of the right bottom petal, and filtering the flower through the paint daubs effect on Adobe Photoshop 2020. The image in grayscale is also used on the second interior title page.

"God is love"
–1 John 4:8

For my children and grandchildren

You are loved by God no matter what.
May you know love,
Grow in love,
And show love to others.
– Becca Ellis

Contents

Introduction   13

Part One – Wounding the Wounded
1. Sitting on the Throne   27
2. Choosing Rules Over Relationship   35
3. Just Do It   41
4. The Problem is in Your Head   47
5. The Paradox   53

Part Two – Understanding Ourselves
6. Brain Basics   65
7. A Tale of Three Babies   73
8. The Heart of the Matter   83
9. Living Life with a Different Nervous System   93

Part Three – A New Spiritual Practice
10. A Way Forward   101
11. Befriending our Protectors   109
12. Befriending Our Exiles   125
13. Guiding Principles for Building Relationships   137

Part Four – Loving Others as We Love Ourselves

14. Seasons of Loss	145
15. The Agony of Betrayal	157
16. A New Perspective on Addiction	171
17. The Emotional Impact of Physical and Mental Illness	187
18. From Exhortation to Transformation	201

Appendix A:
Restoring Relationship: A New Spiritual Practice 207

Appendix B:
Glossary of Key Terms 213

Acknowledgments 217
Endnotes 221

RESTORING

Relationship

Introduction

Despair was creeping into every corner of Ashley's[*] life, like fog blanketing the landscape, obscuring light and color. As her husband became more distant and preoccupied, Ashley grew more anxious and desperate to figure out why the relationship she thought would last for a lifetime seemed to be dying a slow and painful death. She hoped her church community would be a source of support, but when she met with various leaders they gave pat answers or canned advice. She left those encounters feeling worse, increasingly convinced that it was her fault her marriage was in trouble. On Sundays she looked at all of the people around her joyfully worshipping and wondered if she was the only one struggling. On one level she knew other people were dealing with challenges, but in her heart she felt like a failure. After all, if she was the wife she was "supposed" to be, her husband would not be so distant. She tried everything to get his attention, and the harder she tried, the more she felt him slipping away. She believed his rejection was proof that she really *was* unlovable. The shame provoked by the belief that she was unlovable silenced

---

[*] All names have been changed to protect privacy.

her, sending her in a downward spiral of isolation and loneliness. It became too painful to reach out to people. Despite sharing her struggles with her group leader and pastor, when she stopped going to church, no one reached out to her.

Why do people seeking support and healing in the Church sometimes leave feeling more broken than when they arrived? Why isn't the Christian community a place where people can consistently experience freedom from the myriad issues plaguing them? Why do we talk so much about love, but often fail to be loving?

As Jesus prepared his disciples for his departure he said, "Love each other as I have loved you" (John 15:12). Jesus showed us the fullness of God's love. There were no preconditions, no limits, no "insiders" and "outsiders." Love was freely given, available to each person in their particular circumstances. When Christian communities are not reliably a source of this kind of love, we have a problem. We know that loving the way Jesus calls us to love requires transformation. There are obstacles to loving as he taught us to love. But despite a plethora of resources, many continue to struggle, and transformation seems to be an elusive ideal. Is loving like Jesus loves us just impossible?

Jesus would not have launched a revolution and handed the mission over to his followers if we were not capable of carrying it out. N.T. Wright asserts that the focus of the Sermon on the Mount is not ethics; it is about *mission*. "The point is that *God's kingdom is being launched on earth as it is in heaven, and the way it will happen is by God working through people…*"[1] God works through people as we love one another. But we are not very good at it. As a result, we settle for less than Jesus wants for us.

Introduction

Wrestling with the same issues over and over, desperately trying to keep one's head above the raging water of emotional distress day after day, and slapping band-aids on gaping wounds is not consistent with the Good News Jesus came to proclaim. I return over and over again to the passage in Luke's Gospel where Jesus quotes from the book of Isaiah to describe his ministry.

"The Spirit of the Lord is on me, because he has anointed me to preach good news to the poor. He has sent me to *proclaim freedom* for the prisoners and recovery of sight for the blind, to *release the oppressed*, to proclaim the year of the Lord's favor" (Luke 4:18-19). The poor, the captives, the blind and the oppressed would be freed – released from the constraints that block their ability to live the life for which they were created. There are many levels of healing implied in these verses, and surely emotional and relational healing are among them.

When I read the proclamation of Jesus' ministry of freedom for the poor, the captives, the blind, and the oppressed I relate these verses to what I have seen people experience in their relationships with God, others, and themselves. Sadly, the vision is often not realized. In this passage we hear Jesus' heart for people. While Jesus is speaking especially of physical infirmities, his healing power extends to emotional and psychological health. Yet, relationships are often too fraught with difficulties, blocking the loving connection that is our deepest need. Despite an overwhelming amount of available information, a great deal of ignorance abounds about the underlying causes of emotional and relational distress. Many people feel trapped in the prison of patterns that they can see and even articulate, leading to hopelessness and despair. The degree of difficulty leaves many feeling oppressed, burdened by worries, harassed by an ongoing internal critical dialog and fearful of taking a stand for themselves. This is not life in the kingdom! This state of affairs does not reflect the freedom Jesus proclaimed.

Jesus taught that the greatest commandment is to "love the Lord your God with all your heart and with all your soul and with all your mind" and said there is a second commandment "like" the first – to "love your neighbor as yourself" (Matthew 22:37-39). In Paul's letter to the Galatians he asserted "the entire law is fulfilled in keeping this one command: 'Love your neighbor as yourself'" (Galatians 5:14). I believe Jesus provided this focus because relationship is the means by which we attain the freedom and healing he proclaims. When we are hurting, we need loving relationships. Persistent challenges rob us of joy and peace, even calling into question some of our deeply held beliefs – that God loves us unconditionally and personally, that we matter, and that God hears our cries. The "valley of the shadow of death" (Psalm 23:4, KJV) is a tender, sacred place. When we are traveling this difficult path, loving relationships provide a container for our wounded hearts. We need to be held in times of adversity. The psalmist wrote, "Into your hands I commit my spirit; deliver me, Lord, my faithful God" (Psalm 31:5). Jesus echoed these words with his last breath (Luke 23:46).

God calls us to be God's hands, reaching out to offer a safe and trustworthy connection when someone is caught up in the whirlwind of a trying time. Through relationship, Jesus' followers fulfill their primary calling – to continue the work of bringing God's kingdom to the world. Yet, relationships are fraught with challenges.

Introduction

We need a way to restore relationship. It is the thread running through all of our challenges and the single most important thing we need in order to thrive personally and as a community of faith. *We need more than exhortation; we need transformation.* We need a spiritual practice that provides a path from broken relationships to loving relationships. There are many wonderful devotional books to strengthen our connection to God, and an abundance of resources focused on relationships between people – couples, parents and children, etc. But one dimension of the Great Commandment has gotten far less attention – our relationship with ourselves. And that is where connection must begin.

Restoring relationship begins within ourselves because the constraints to the loving relationships for which we were created lie within ourselves. We were created in God's image (Genesis 1:27), in the image of the God who "is love" (1 John 4:8), so if we have difficulty loving one another it seems likely that something inside of us is blocking our love. Imagine what could happen if we had a way to remove the obstacles, to release the constraints to love in all its beautiful forms!

When we turn our attention to these obstacles, we have the opportunity to release the constraints to our natural ability to love. I have seen the power of this approach to healing since shifting the focus of my psychotherapy practice to the Internal Family Systems (IFS) model.[2] The IFS model was developed by Dr. Richard Schwartz, a brilliant psychotherapist who was determined to figure out a way for clients to heal. He was not satisfied with coping; he wanted clients to thrive. He trained in many different modalities, all of which offered something helpful. Yet, he still did not see the outcomes he hoped for with clients. With tenacious curiosity, he decided to "listen carefully and trust what my clients were telling me about their inner worlds."[3] He discovered that the dysfunctional behaviors and distressing symptoms bringing clients to therapy – the things that were blocking their ability to thrive – were actually strategies or coping mechanisms that had a *positive intention*.

For example, in working with a client who cut herself, he learned that cutting was a protective strategy.[4] A protective strategy is adopted to prevent something terrible from happening. In this case, a part of the client – what we call a "protector" – was trying to keep her from being abused and from doing something that might endanger her following the abuse. It had a positive intention – it did not want her to suffer far worse pain than it inflicted by cutting her. Despite the extreme way it chose to protect her, the protector meant well. When Dr. Schwartz shifted his approach from trying to *control* the part doing the cutting to *connecting* with it, he felt appreciation for the heroic role it played.[5] This was the beginning of an approach rooted in relationship.

As Dr. Schwartz continued to listen with open curiosity, he found that all of his clients had different personalities within them, some of whom seemed child-like, others who were critical or perfectionistic, and still others who were impulsive and even destructive. Clients typically referred to these different personalities as "parts" of themselves.[6]

In addition to recognizing the presence of various parts in the inner worlds of his clients – what Dr. Schwartz came to call *family members* – he was stunned to discover that there was always a leader of this inner family, no matter what clients experienced in life.[7] He was surprised because many theories of psychotherapy

Introduction

believe that without "good enough" early experiences with caregivers we can lack essential qualities for healthy functioning. His discovery is much more congruent with the biblical truth that we are created in God's image; we are image-bearers and the image of God cannot be obliterated by anything. Dr. Schwartz discovered that the leader of the inner family had qualities such as compassion, clarity, curiosity and calm – qualities we recognize as attributes of God. Ultimately, he realized that when the leader of this inner family could connect with different family members in their various roles, the fears and burdens that drove their behavior could be resolved. Loving relationships were the answer to his question of how to help his clients heal.

At this point you might wonder, despite superficial congruence with biblical truth, whether this is more of a psychological, rather than biblical, approach to healing. But all truth is God's truth. God created humans as psychological, social, emotional, and spiritual beings. We learn God's truth by reading God's word *and* by observing how humans interact with one another, with God, and with themselves. The more I have studied, experienced, and worked with this model, the more I have seen that this method is profoundly biblical. I will share more about the integration of IFS and biblical and theological truth later in this book. At this point, I encourage you to consider how my client Cindy's story illustrates the power of this approach for healing.

Cindy reached out to me at a time of crisis in her life. Her husband of over 30 years had left her for another woman. He was a member of the clergy in their church and was fired from his position as a result of his affair. She was overwhelmed by intense grief, fear about her future, questions of self-worth, and unrelenting second-guessing about what she could have done differently to save the marriage. As she shared her story, I heard fear of the judgment she would suffer. I heard her believe the lie that it must be her fault that her husband turned to another woman. I heard despair over the futility of trying her best to follow the rules, to live a godly life. Sometimes she would say, "I just need to get over this." She was beset by troubling beliefs about her lack of worth and "failure" as a wife and mother. The deep distress she felt prompted protective members of her inner family to work to try to keep the pain from overwhelming her. While well-intentioned, protectors block access to the qualities we possess as image-bearers. They usurp the leadership role when they work to control things or by attempting to numb pain. Again, they mean well, but they push past the leader of the system and, consequently, block the leader's resources. In order to heal the pain, Cindy learned to start by developing relationships with these hard-working protectors. As she earned their trust, they relaxed and allowed her to regain the leadership role. She was then able to connect with the tender, wounded parts of her, offering the love and compassion they needed in order to heal. As a result of her inner healing, relationships with many external family members improved, her social circle expanded, and she felt more capable and successful in her job. The loving relationship she established with inner family members opened more capacity for loving relationships with others and a deeper sense of connection with God.

My goal is to help you learn how to establish this type of loving relationship with your inner family. The spiritual practice of connecting to the different parts of ourselves is a powerful means

Introduction

of transformation, freeing us to love as we are called to do.

Before we learn about this spiritual practice, we will tackle some critical issues. The first and the subject of Part I is the common reactions to distress encountered by people in the Church. Most of these reactions are well-intentioned approaches, but they inadvertently contribute to the emotional and relational distress people are experiencing. The strategies people use in an effort to be helpful often break relationship because *they are rooted in fear, not love*. We fear vulnerability, and it is very vulnerable to go through a time of distress or to walk with someone who is. Most of our reactive responses to adversity reflect a desire to avoid our own and others' vulnerability. Our fear of vulnerability blocks our capacity to connect with one another when we need it most. Reflecting on the way Jesus embraced vulnerability throughout his life, most vividly on the cross, helps us realize that turning toward our vulnerability is a key step in healing.

Turning toward vulnerability is not our natural, instinctive response. The fear we feel is real and it is powerful. We cannot simply talk ourselves out of being afraid because our early experiences of vulnerability exert a powerful influence on a subconscious level. Humans are especially vulnerable at birth and highly susceptible to environmental influences that impact our ability to connect. In Part II we will explore the basics of "interpersonal neurobiology" to better understand the importance of relationship for well-being, and the influence of development on how we relate to ourselves and others. I promise it will not be too technical! Understanding how development shapes our functioning helps to remove the constraints to our natural capacity for compassion. We gain important perspective in recognizing all of us carry experiences of vulnerability that shape our response to present circumstances. Accepting our vulnerability and learning to connect with it in gracious, loving ways is an essential aspect of healing. Understanding how the human brain and mind develop gives us insight into the roots of emotional and relational distress and helps with comprehending why some of the traditional approaches to "helping" can actually wound the already wounded. With greater compassion for vulnerability and the fear it provokes, we will then turn back to the spiritual practice that enables us to embrace and transform our fear.

In Part III we will delve more deeply into the IFS model, exploring the integration with Christianity, and demonstrating how a new spiritual practice based on the model restores relationship with ourselves, one another, and God. You will have an opportunity to learn about your inner family. Exercises guide you in a new spiritual practice to release constraints to the innate qualities you possess as an image-bearer. Engaging in this new practice restores your leadership of your inner family. The new spiritual practice is rooted in guiding principles for restoring relationship, a framework for transforming fear into love. The most important guiding principle of all is "there is no fear in love. But perfect love drives out fear…" (1 John 4:18). Fear is driven out not because it is judged or unwelcome, but because it is embraced, understood, and transformed.

Finally, in Part IV we will examine some of the most common causes of distress prompting people to seek help. Spending time considering the impact of loss, betrayal, addiction, and the emotional impact of physical and mental illness helps build an understanding of typical responses to these complex causes of distress.

Introduction

Exercises will deepen connection with parts that naturally have a reaction to distress. Each topic will provide an opportunity to practice the new spiritual discipline. Gaining experience with this practice will equip you to offer the relationship that heals – to live out the heart of the Great Commandment.

Part One

WOUNDING THE WOUNDED

Chapter One
SITTING ON THE THRONE

Ella looked forward to the time each week when she would gather with the other women on the Bible study leadership team. It was a time of prayer and study, of laughter and sometimes tears – a time of connection. The meeting with the other leaders helped her prepare for her role as a children's teacher. She loved teaching children about Jesus; her face lit up as the little ones arrived for the day. She was creative and nurturing and fun. Ella brought all of her love and skills to the children's program of her Bible study – until she got divorced.

The divorce happened at a time when divorce was much less common and much more controversial in the church than it is today. The organization sponsoring the Bible study did not allow divorcees to serve in leadership roles. At a time when she was navigating one of the most difficult experiences of her life, she was cut off from one of her most important sources of support, the other leaders in her study.

What message did this woman who was so devoted to children receive?

You are damaged, unfit to teach children.

Imagine being Ella, receiving the phone call from someone she thought was her friend telling her she was no longer welcome in their group. Can you feel your heart start to pound? Do you want to hang up as quickly as possible because the lump in your throat is making it impossible to speak? Does the shame of being cast out flood your face?

I wonder how it felt when she took her children to church. I suspect some of the people there judged her for her divorce as well. It is a testimony to the depth of her faith that Ella did not leave her spiritual community despite experiencing judgment at a very vulnerable time in her life. She turned her energy toward her own children, driving a great distance to take them to Christian schools and making sure when she had grandchildren they too had opportunities to learn about Jesus. Eventually she found a new Bible study, and she approached the leaders to see if a class could start in her part of town so she could get back to serving the children. While in her 70's, Ella ran her own business, was actively involved in all aspects of her family life, and served once again as a children's teacher. Despite being diagnosed with cancer that required surgery and chemotherapy, she continued to serve until she was near the end of her life.

Ella asked me to speak at her memorial service and during our final visit together I hoped to get a sense for what she would want me to say. I already had a passage in mind from Proverbs 31. Verses in that passage such as, "She gets up while it is still night; she provides food for her family..." "She opens her arms to the poor and extends her hands to the needy," and especially, "She is clothed with strength and dignity...She speaks with wisdom, and faithful instruction is on her tongue" reflect the life she led, and the woman she was (Proverbs 31:15-26). I was hoping she would approve of the idea of building my comments around that passage, but I never had a chance to mention it to her.

At a time when Ella was just hours from death she told me she felt utterly worthless.

I was heartbroken. How was it possible that someone so dedicated to her faith did not heal? What was missing?

The church told her she was a failure because of divorce, and the shame she felt silenced her. Rather than having a caring community to support her through one of the most difficult seasons of her life, she was left to fend for herself: left with her shame, left with her sense of failure, left alone. Instead of love she received judgment.

When a hurting person is met with judgment they often believe they deserve it. Picture Ella, hearing from leaders in her Bible study that she is unfit to teach children, and then hearing her own inner critic saying, "See? You *are* worthless." I imagine a woman seeing critical faces and hearing critical voices wherever she turns. I can feel the cringing inside, the flush on my cheeks, the pain of shame. It is utterly isolating. It makes me want to run away. In Ella's case, she soldiered on, the picture of courage. And the picture of tragedy, because her wound never healed. The belief that she was worthless stayed with her until the very end of her life. In her case the Christian community that exists to proclaim the unconditional love of Jesus, the inexhaustible forgiveness that is available to all, and the safety of knowing all are welcome, opted instead for judgment.

I wish the kind of judgment Ella faced were a relic of our past. I wish hurting people would no longer be met with judgment when they come to church hoping for understanding and compassion. I wish our bias toward judgment were not so strong.

Why would a community that follows a God who "is love" (1 John 4:8), a community instructed to "love each other deeply" (1 Peter 4:8), and exhorted to patiently bear "with one another in love" (Ephesians 4:2), opt for judgment instead of love? What is powerful enough to push out the love that is the testimony to the profound mystery of God dwelling within each of us?

Fear.

Fear is the emotion that prompts us to turn to judgment. Fear is, unfortunately, potent enough to block love. Fear motivates our protective strategies, blocking our heart and shifting the focus from relationship to rules.

Think of the many interactions Jesus had with the Pharisees and other teachers of the law. They were fearful of his influence, fearful of his lavish grace in welcoming all people among his followers, and fearful of his emphasis on meeting needs over following the letter of the law.[8] Some of them feared him so much they plotted to arrest and kill him (Matthew 26:4), the ultimate act of judgment.

Something about lavish love and grace scares us. There is something deep in us that prefers the certainty of rules, of categories that define who is "in" and who is "out" even when we are confronted by someone who is hurting. There is a form of safety in defining these categories; it quells some of the fear prompted by openness. We wonder what will happen if we are too open, too gracious. It is unsettling. I believe if we are honest with ourselves, we will realize the extent to which we operate from fear rather than love.

Author Gregory Boyd asserts that judgment is the original sin:

"Our fundamental sin is that we place ourselves in the position of God and divide the world between what we judge to be good and what we judge to be evil."[9] We "embrace a moral system" focusing on "being good people in contrast to all those who are evil." Jesus challenged this tendency when the religious leaders brought a woman to him who had been caught committing adultery (John 8:3-4). They felt entirely justified in judging and condemning her, but Jesus turned their attention back to their own sin. We trade what should be our role, being loving, for what belongs to God alone, judging. And the real problem with this is that we derive our worth from doing so. We seem to get a sense of worth, however fleeting and false, from judging another, from finding them to be "less than" in some way. We inflate our sense of worth by deflating another's. This helps to quell the fear most of us have at some level that we are unworthy.

It is important to distinguish discernment from judgment. Discerning good and evil is something we are called to do. However, when we judge we are "drawing conclusions about people"[10] based on our determination of good and evil. We muscle our way into God's position when we move from discernment to judgment. A conclusion was drawn about Ella based on her divorce. Drawing conclusions about others reveals that we have the wrong motive; our motive is to judge, not love. Whether we say it out loud, or think it to ourselves, judgment creates a chasm between the judge and the judged. We, the judge, avoid, disregard, even shun the hurting person.

The next time you are out in public or sitting in a church service, see whether you notice the presence of a judgmental member of your inner family making statements such as:

Restoring Relationship

"That person is obese because they lack discipline."

"Their son was arrested; they must have really messed up as parents."

"Her husband left her. He's such a great guy; she must have done something to deserve that."

Notice the impact of these thoughts on your desire to connect with the person. When thoughts like these surface, a judgmental part of you has taken over leadership of your inner family. If you wonder whether your thoughts, actions, or behaviors really reflect judgment versus love, check your heart. How open is your heart to the other person? Do you feel compassion for their struggle? Do you feel like you are members of the same community or does judgment, however subtle, render the person "other?"

Judgment puts people in categories. It builds walls. It breaks the unity that Jesus said should be a hallmark of the Christian community. In his final prayer on the night of the Last Supper Jesus said our unity reflects the love that binds us together – and unity is a compelling message to a hurting world (John 17:23).

Some will argue that these categories are necessary, that they help the Christian community stay true to biblical values and principles. However, it is important to examine the motive behind the categories. Is it love, or is it judgment?

If we want the Christian community to be a safe place for hurting people we should be less concerned with judgment and more concerned about love. "Dear friends, let us love one another, for love comes from God…if we love one another, God lives in us and his love is made complete in us…There is no fear in love. But perfect love drives out fear…" (1 John 4:7-21). When we turn toward the parts of us holding fear, connect with those parts, and reassure them, we open space for grace and love. If a struggling person is met with love, it is far more likely that they will be able to grapple with any changes they need to make or actions they need to take. Love has a way of removing the barriers to clarity about our circumstances. Love creates the safety we need in order to be honest with ourselves. Love needs to be our first and consistent response. Jesus shows us that, and he also shows us that he had little tolerance for religious leaders who put judgment ahead of love.

Consider our tendency to judge in the context of the commandment to love God, one another, and ourselves. We break our connection with one another when we focus on who is in and who is out, whose behavior is acceptable and whose is not, who is worthy of love and who is not. It is destructive to individuals and communities and to our witness in the world. And it breaks God's heart.

Believe me, I am not judging the tendency to judge! We all do it. Jesus provided a graphic illustration to make sure we would remember to focus on our own deficiencies rather than someone else's. "Why do you look at the speck of sawdust in someone else's eye and pay no attention to the plank in your own eye?" (Luke 6:41-42, TNIV) We have a plank in our eye – some issue that is unresolved – and we ignore it so we can focus on a speck in someone else's eye. That takes some effort! We actually put a fair amount of energy into our judgments. Judging others is not our mission in the world, but it is one of the things people associate most with Christians.[11] Judgment persists because of fear. Turning toward the plank in our eye, toward our fear, is the first step in the new spiritual practice that removes the constraints to love.

Chapter Two
Choosing Rules Over Relationship

The monitors beeped rhythmically in the cool room full of neonatal intensive care bassinets. A tiny little girl lay in one of them with multiple tubes snaking around her body. A nurse was in the room, but no one was visiting Lucy. Her parents were with her healthy twin brother, delighting in the fact that they had a son. They were told that Lucy might not survive.

So they prayed.

What prayer was spoken over the little girl struggling for her life? Her parents prayed, "Lord, please take her if she is not going to be a good Christian." Her parents did not want her to survive if she was not going to be a "good Christian." Over the years, Lucy was told repeatedly that this was their prayer.

And she got the message.

Be "good" or you are worthless. Be "good" or you don't deserve to live. You do not automatically deserve love; you have to earn it.

Being a "good" Christian meant following the rules, and there were lots of rules: rules about not being silly and playful, rules about not making Daddy angry, rules about making sure she was not too much trouble, rules about keeping her feelings to herself, rules about keeping quiet even when adults hurt her badly.

Lucy knew about God. God was the angry one who was never pleased with her, never satisfied that she was good enough. God terrified her. Her parents seemed a lot like God; they were often angry and displeased and scary.

Certain that both God and her parents were watching carefully to see if she was "good enough," Lucy became an extremely hard working perfectionist. She cut herself off from her own emotions because the dual messages she had received since she was born were that emotions are messy and that being orderly, quiet and compliant was equal to being "good." She tried to become someone who would please both God and her parents. She knew it was up to her to figure out how to please them, what it meant to be good; if she didn't, she didn't deserve to live. She felt abandoned by God and her parents. Her loneliness and fear were intense.

The tragic irony is that Lucy's parents thought that their prayer *pleased* God. They thought they were being "good" Christians. Rather than being motivated by love, her parents focused on following rules. We see from Lucy's experience that when rules are the focus, fear dominates. She was filled with the fear that if she did not live up to the expectation of being a "good Christian" she might as well die. I suspect fear was also the motivation behind her parents' prayer.

Recall the verses Jesus quoted to describe his ministry. "The Spirit of the Lord is on me, because he has anointed me to preach good news to the poor. He has sent me to proclaim freedom for the prisoners and recovery of sight for the blind, to release the oppressed…" (Luke 4:18-19). Jesus promises healing, freedom, and release. He did not come to bind people to a new set of rules; he came to free us from bondage to a system that provokes fear and shame so we could enjoy the loving relationship that was always God's desire – so we can live out our purpose as image-bearers. Jesus emphasized *faith* and he challenged religious leaders whose rules left people in bondage. As Bonhoeffer wrote, "Jesus calls [people] not to a new religion but to life."[12]

Lucy needed relationship, not rules. She needed parents whose unconditional love sent the message that she was worthy of love no matter what. Instead, she got a set of rules that were impossible to live up to. She learned that God is a harsh father who is watching closely for any transgression. Lucy internalized painful beliefs and feelings because of the emphasis on working for God's approval. Despite the fact that she clung to her faith and remained in the church, she was reminded over and over that God did not really love her. She knew the things she learned about grace and forgiveness did not apply to her.

Why do we opt for rules over relationship?

We explored one of the reasons in Chapter One. Taking over the job that belongs only to God, becoming judges instead of lovers, fuels a focus on rules. Just as fear motivates judgment, it also motivates us to trade relationship for rules. When fear is in charge, it can prompt us to huddle inside our Christian bubble and worry about aspects of the culture that do not seem consistent with biblical values. Rather than feeling confident that we can gather with open arms, welcoming everyone who wants to experience the unconditional love of Jesus, we build walls out of rules, essentially deciding who is, and is not, worthy of love. Our fear reflects the sad fact that it is difficult to fully trust that love is what we all need; we opt for rules to control what seems chaotic and uncertain.

Rules do seem to bring order to the chaos and uncertainty. They give us a sense of control. They calm our fears. So it makes sense that we would focus on rules. We want reassurance that if we abide by them we will pass the test. We will be found worthy, which is one of our most fundamental needs. It remains so difficult for most of us to believe, on a gut and heart level, that we are worthy simply because we exist. When the Pharisees grumbled about Jesus' habit of welcoming sinners and eating with them (Luke 15:2), Jesus reminded them that each person is precious and worthy of his attention. "Rejoice with me; I have found my lost sheep" (Luke 15:6). Too often our focus shifts from Jesus' loving gaze to the rules that provide a poor substitute for his assurance of our worthiness.

The emphasis on rules tends to lead to a focus on behavior. After all, if our job is to determine whether someone is a "good Christian" evaluating their behavior makes sense. We like to turn to the "sin lists"[13] as a resource and we have a tendency to prioritize some sins over others. I am not implying that we should ignore what Scripture teaches regarding things that are life-giving and consistent with being a follower of Jesus. But we cannot start with outcomes. Behavior is an *outcome* of complex processes that we will explore in Parts II and III. Focusing on behavior puts us right back in the judgment seat, back in the position of evaluating someone according to a checklist. That plank is back in our eye, and we are trying to see around it to find the speck in the other person's eye.

The question for anyone who wants to be a source of healing is whether we offer *religious rules* to the hurting person, or *loving relationship*. Do we "diagnose" their struggle as a failure to live according to the rules, or do we understand that the most important thing we have to offer is relationship, the message that we are with them, not above them? "Only love, given without hesitation and without conditions, can ever motivate people to trust us enough to invite us to speak into their lives in the first place."[14] When someone is struggling, our tendency to rush in with rules and advice can inadvertently contribute to their distress. Psalm 46 provides guidance about what is needed during troubled times. "God is our refuge and strength, an ever-present help in trouble…[God] says, 'Be still, and know that I am God'" (Psalm 46:1,10). When we lead our inner family, drawing on our innate resources as image-bearers along with the power of the Holy Spirit, we can be calm and confident in connecting with a hurting person. Our presence allows them to be still, to feel God's presence, opening the possibility of authentic relationship.

If we focus first on rules and behavior, people will feel the need to perform and will hide their authentic self and their real struggles. Many people show up to their Bible study, small group, or worship service wearing a costume to cover something they learned is unacceptable in their spiritual community. As long as the issues remain hidden, there is no possibility of healing. Healing can only begin when people receive the kind of love Jesus shows us, love that is not based on performance.* Love provides the balm, the safe holding, and the security necessary for healing to happen.

---

*   For an excellent example, see the story of Jesus' interaction with the Samaritan woman at the well in John 4:1-42.

Lucy reached a point where she was tired of hiding, tired of the relentless drive to perform, and tired of living out of fear and shame. She embarked on a very courageous journey of healing. Over time, the energy that used to fuel her drive for perfection was freed up to fuel her entrepreneurial ventures, social connections, and participation in ministries where she could extend compassion to others. Her vision of God as a harsh and demanding father was transformed as she healed; she now experiences God as unconditionally loving and gracious. Her journey took many years of intentional effort. It was not smooth or linear; it was full of boulders and switchbacks. This type of journey takes patience and persistence both from the one who is healing and those who are supporting the healing. Sadly, patience and persistence can be in short supply in a culture with a "just do it" mentality.

Chapter Three
JUST DO IT

I read a story about a woman who gave her pastor a slip of paper every week after his sermon.[15] Each week there was a different number on the paper. Sometimes it grew larger until it was a fairly big number. Other times it was smaller, as low as two. It was the number of days since the woman last cut herself.

The woman shared that she had a long history of abuse, of being beaten and neglected, and the pastor acknowledged how difficult it would be for her to believe that "God loves her unconditionally, without reservation, without her having to do anything to earn it."[16] He went on to use the Parable of the Prodigal Son (Luke 15:11-32) to illustrate how our version of our story does not match God's version.[17] After squandering his inheritance the younger son journeys home certain that he is no longer worthy to be called his father's son. The older brother views his work as slavery and accuses his father of being unfair. In both cases, the father had a very different perspective about his sons. The younger son was welcomed home with celebration, and the older son was told "you are always with me, and everything I have is yours."

This interpretation of the well-known parable is insightful. It is striking to see the contrast between each son's version of the story and God's. However, the pastor's assertion that "we *create hell* whenever we *fail to trust* God's retelling of our story"[18] caught my attention. The implication is that we *freely choose* our version of the story or God's. What happens when a person who is cutting herself to bear the pain of living hears she is *creating hell* by failing to trust God? Self-harm is an adaptation to pain. This woman *experienced* hell; she did not create it by failing to trust. Adversity, particularly when it occurs early in life, undermines our ability to trust. It also leaves a legacy of powerlessness, blocking the confidence needed to make choices freely. The kind of adversity that leads to self-harm often burdens a person with shame and a sense of worthlessness. Burdens must be healed in order to restore our freedom to trust and to choose. Until healing happens, we see ourselves and others through the veil of shame and worthlessness, obscuring God's vision of our lives.

The idea that we should "just trust" is pretty pervasive. For example, I noticed this statement in an ad for a book. "What determines whether God's healing power is experienced within our hearts and minds is whether we trust God and open our hearts to him."[19]

Just trust and you will be free. Trust, and you will experience God's "healing power."

We want it to be that simple. On one hand, it is the best news in the Good News – that we really do not have to do anything to earn God's love, to step into his version of our story. Yet, that one step can seem like taking a leap over the Grand Canyon because it requires *trust*. For many people, especially people like the woman in the story, trust is not simple and it is not easy. It is a monumental challenge that has nothing to do with choice.

During the earliest hours, days, and months of their lives, babies take in information that affects their ability to trust. Life experiences yield more information that combine to create a narrative about the world that tells the person whether it is safe to trust. For far too many, the world is not safe and it is not trustworthy. And they certainly did not *choose* to live in that kind of world.

When we tell distressed people that they "just need to trust," we invalidate their concerns.

We also deny the complexity of their challenges when we ask, "How could someone choose another way with a universe of love and joy and peace right in front of them?"[20] We imply that they are blind to what is obvious, that there is a simple solution and we know it but they do not. We might think our approach is loving, but it does not build a relationship or foster connection.

Can you recall a time when you were stuck – caught up in a dilemma that did not seem to be solvable? If so, bring your attention to what is happening inside of you as you remember. Maybe there is frustration; can you feel it in your body? Are there thoughts connected to the frustration? Something like, "You should be able to figure this out. Why can't you just accept what others seem to be able to believe?" Perhaps you notice grief, the heaviness and gloom that will not dissipate.

What if someone you turned to for help said, "You just need to trust..." Trust God's plan. Trust that it will be OK. Trust that God wants the best for you.

How do those statements feel as you recall your dilemma? Does it feel like the other person really understands what you are experiencing? Do you think they are available to walk with you along the twisting path when the destination is not clear?

It would not feel that way to me. Those "just trust" statements feel more like a door closing in my face, shutting me out from a place where I feel welcome, cutting me off from the companionship I need during a challenging time.

If we can resist the temptation to tell someone what they need or what they should do – if we can stay in a place of not knowing, a place of humility and genuine curiosity – then we have the potential to connect in a way that can foster healing.

Unfortunately, it seems that the Christian community has adopted Nike's slogan "Just do it." Just trust. Just change. Just obey. Just stop it.

When someone is struggling with an addiction, they are told "don't drink; don't use." When there is violence in relationships, people are told to "stop being angry." When a grieving person is sad longer than tolerable (which is not long at all in our culture), they are told to "get over it" and move on. We confront challenges by raising our arm in a "stop" gesture – sending a very clear message that we cannot tolerate the messiness of unresolved issues.

It is so difficult to stay with someone, right beside them, listening and offering presence, when we think that it is our job to tell them what they need to hear. We are action-oriented. We want people to take steps, set resolutions, and get busy making the changes we know they need to make. Somewhere along the way we traded Jesus' approach for a much less humble one.

Jesus offers presence. "Come to me, all you who are weary and burdened, and I will give you rest. Take my yoke upon you and learn from me, for I am gentle and humble in heart, and you will find rest for your souls" (Matthew 11:28-29).

Jesus offers *rest* when we are weary and burdened. When we are struggling we need to pause in the presence of a gentle and humble person to quiet the noise, to be still, to be able to listen and learn and find our way forward.

If we think our responsibility is to tell the other person what they need it will be more difficult *not* to have answers. It will be more difficult *not* to know the solution to a particular person's dilemma. It will be more difficult to quiet ourselves, to be still ourselves, to be in a state of calm curiosity when we are in the presence of distress.

The only way we can shift from a "just do it" advice-giving approach is if we remember what Jesus offers when we are weary and burdened. Jesus offers relationship grounded in presence. Astonishingly, the image he gives us of the relationship is not hierarchical. He says, "take my yoke upon you," inviting us to come alongside him, to walk together, to learn from his presence.

In his humility, Jesus comes to us not as one who is going to lord over us, eager to tell us all the ways we need to change. He invites us into his presence because the first and most important gift we can give or receive is love. Love is the medium that gives anything else we have to offer – words of wisdom, encouragement for the hard work of growth and change, prayers of support – the desired effect. It helps to remember Paul's vivid language about the priority of love: "If I have the gift of prophecy and can fathom all mysteries and all knowledge, and if I have a faith that can move mountains, but do not have love, I am nothing" (1 Corinthians 13:2).

If we start to observe ourselves we will probably notice that words, the "just do it" kinds of statements, are reactions to someone's distress. At best they are well-intentioned strategies to offer something of use, and at worst they distance us from someone or some situation we find overwhelming. These statements are often our default response.

Cultivating loving presence, the medium for the true healing Jesus came to proclaim, requires a change when we have a "just do it" mindset. Please know that I am not suggesting that you "just change" your method of relating to hurting people and yourself! I will be providing a model in Part III that helps us understand the impulse to tell people what to do or what to believe, and also gives us a way of being in loving relationship with ourselves and others so we can experience the rest and healing Jesus offers.

Chapter Four
THE PROBLEM IS IN YOUR HEAD

I watched a video of a pastor who challenged the "just do it" focus on behavior. He hoped to offer a better approach than what he called the, "Don't worry; be happy!" message so often given to people in distress.[21] I was intrigued, especially because he addressed his wife's anxiety with his approach. Many of the clients I have seen over the years are primarily struggling with anxiety. It can be especially difficult for a Christian to acknowledge their anxiety because they are frequently told "Do not be anxious about anything…" (Philippians 4:6), the biblical version of "Don't worry; be happy!"

Instead of behavior, the pastor advocated focusing on underlying beliefs, asserting "What people believe [about God] shows up in what they do" – in the "fruit" they produce. Therefore, if his wife's "fruit" is anxiety, the problem must be with her beliefs about God. His thesis was, essentially, that believing lies about God leads to anxiety, but believing the truth about God dispels anxiety. Thus, he illustrated a process of identifying distorted beliefs and replacing them with true beliefs, which yielded, at least temporarily, relief from the anxiety his wife was experiencing.

Finally! Something pretty straightforward that is easy to remember: replace false beliefs with the truth.

Not so fast. Beware of strategies that oversimplify. Thoughts are just one of the elements present during times of anxiety or other distress. If we focus all of our attention on thoughts, we might as well be playing "whack-a-mole." Something else *will* pop up!

The clue that this thought-based approach is an oversimplification is in the pastor's own statement – "This is a daily struggle, to continue to remember the truths of God as revealed in Jesus Christ, for me; I'm sure it is for you too."

Is this the best we can offer? A daily struggle, a wrestling match where we try to pin down "false" beliefs?

I do not believe this is what Jesus intends for us. If we adopt this strategy, we are settling for something far short of fully experiencing what Jesus offers. The pastor was correct in shifting the sole focus from behavior, and it is true that beliefs are an important indicator of our well-being, but he fell short of focusing on what Jesus tells us makes all the difference.

Relationship.

The fruit we bear is not simply a reflection of beliefs, which are often transient or even conflicted. The fruit we bear reflects the quality of our relationships with Jesus, with one another and, very importantly, with ourselves.

Jesus said, "Remain in me, as I also remain in you" (John 15:4). "As the Father has loved me, so have I loved you. Now remain in my love" (John 15:9). In the next several verses, Jesus repeatedly connects an obedient life to our relationships. He draws a circle, connecting love for him, love for one another, and the obedience and "fruit" that flows from a life grounded in this loving communion. One does not exist without the other.

The loving relationship that is central in Jesus' teaching is about far more than beliefs. When we focus on beliefs *about* Jesus, rather than our relationship *with* Jesus, we lose the most important dimension of relationship – the emotional experience. I think it is fair to say that there is far more emphasis in many Christian circles on what we *think* about God than what we *feel* about him. We can hold "correct" beliefs without feeling the love that is our greatest need. In emphasizing beliefs, we have missed, or even cut ourselves off from, loving relationship.

Imagine your closest relationship – with a spouse, a parent, a child, or a dear friend. If you only had your beliefs about that person, would the relationship be as meaningful? What about the times when your heart is warmed by their presence, when your body tingles with excited anticipation of a reunion, when your whole face lights up as you share time together? Do you notice how our emotional experience is grounded in our bodies, and is accompanied by many sensations? This is a "whole body experience" kind of connection. For many of us, the beliefs we have about someone would be fleeting if they were not the *outcome* of the emotional experience.

When we are struggling we need to be held by this kind of "whole body" connection. And we connect through our emotions.[22] Jesus exhorts us to "remain" in him, to remain connected as a branch is to the vine that gives it sustenance (John 15:5), so that we will have continuous access to his love. In the same way, we need to be connected to one another, and to ourselves.

This relationship *does* require something of us daily. Nurturing this connection requires that we bring our attention to all dimensions of our relational life – with God, one another, and ourselves. As we intentionally notice what is happening in our relationships, we can practice being open to it, curious about it, and loving toward it. In doing so, we draw near to it, as Jesus drew near to those who were in need around him. When our heart is open to whatever is happening, we often experience more peace without doing anything else. Presence brings peace because we begin to feel the love that Jesus pours out so freely.

When we are suffering, we not only have distressing thoughts, we are flooded with emotions such as overwhelming anxiety or grief or rage. The more we are caught up in a wave of emotion, the less likely we are to be able to even use the part of our brain involved with thinking. Therefore, when we want to be present for someone who is in distress, the first step of connection is to make room for their emotion. If we bypass it to focus only on beliefs, we are actually sending a message that the emotion is invalid or somehow wrong. Emotions give us important information. They are part of the wonderful brain God created, so ignoring the information or sending a message that the emotion is wrong or bad or inappropriate is not going to provide any lasting benefit. Validating the emotion, which does not require that we understand or agree with it, instead sends a message that we are available to connect and are accepting of the other person's experience.

This is just the first step in a process of being helpful when someone is experiencing distress. My hope is that you are beginning to understand the importance of attending to emotional experience, rather than focusing primarily on thoughts. Focusing solely on beliefs does nothing to heal the underlying cause of the distressing beliefs or the emotions related to them, which is why it can become a daily struggle to challenge distorted beliefs.

Jesus said, "the truth will set you free" (John 8:32). But he did not define truth as a list of correct beliefs. He said, "I am the... truth..." (John 14:6). The truth is a *person* – a person who wants a relationship with us, and shows us what loving relationships look like. He affirmed the greatest commandment, and the one "like it" – to love God, and to love one another as ourselves (Matthew 22:38-39). The "truth" that sets us free is the truth of our most fundamental purpose – to be in loving relationship, to be connected on an emotional, not just intellectual, level. We will explore much more about how this connection sets us free, and how it releases those who are in bondage and in need of healing.

Chapter Five
The Paradox

There is a common thread running through the issues we have just explored: fear of vulnerability.

When we are vulnerable – open, tender, exposed – we can be wounded. Hurting people are vulnerable, and we often feel vulnerable in their presence. It brings up our own times of distress, our own questions and doubts, our own insecurities. And that is not a comfortable place to be. So we resort to a variety of strategies (judgment, legalism, advice giving, challenging distorted beliefs) that we believe will somehow help the other person. Or, at least, these strategies help us stop feeling quite so vulnerable in the face of their challenges.

A friend shared her concern about her husband's increasing anxiety. A variety of significant stressors triggered his early childhood trauma, and he was finding it difficult to eat, sleep, work, and parent their three young children. She was mystified that the simplest task, such as putting the kids in their car seats to take them to school, was beyond his capability. My friend was terrified. Would he lose his job? Would he be like this forever? It felt like she had another young child in her home. Understandably, she tried a few of the strategies we have just discussed, to no avail. His need for comfort was starting to overwhelm her, and she was finding herself wanting to disconnect. She tearfully told me that she was finding it difficult to be around his neediness.

My friend's reaction to her husband's distress was entirely understandable. Theirs is a complex situation with no quick and easy solution. Her fears about her husband's vulnerable emotional state are as natural as her grief about it. We can all resonate with her response. Fear of vulnerability is something we have all experienced.

As normal and understandable as the fear of vulnerability is, it also creates barriers to relationship. Just when my friend's husband most needed her reassuring presence, his vulnerability made her want to disconnect. Paradoxically, we shy away from the very thing that enables us to have our most meaningful relationships. It is just too scary.

But it wasn't always that way. Consider this statement in the Creation story: "The man and his wife were both naked, and they felt no shame" (Genesis 2:25). Beyond just physical nudity, there is a sense that there was no barrier of any kind between Adam and Eve.[23] This is the ideal, that the couple could be vulnerable without shame, without the need to hide.

Why is there a connection between vulnerability and shame, especially when vulnerability was the original, ideal experience in relationship? The connection between vulnerability and shame lies in our *response* to vulnerability.

The openness and authenticity associated with vulnerability in relationships leaves us open to being rejected. When we take the risk to reveal something painful – a sense of helplessness, fear of failure, the torment of temptation to which we repeatedly succumb – what happens when the other person pities us or turns away or gives advice? We feel defective and that provokes shame. So we hide. We do not keep taking the risk of getting hurt; we put on a mask and pretend all is well. But when vulnerability is greeted with acceptance, compassion, validation and understanding, then there is no shame – there is connection. This is true on every level of relationship, with God, one another, and with ourselves.

Jesus redeemed vulnerability. He showed us throughout his life, and most vividly on the cross, that there is no shame in being vulnerable. His example invites us to approach vulnerability with courage rather than fear. Consider the many ways Jesus was vulnerable.

His mother was betrothed but unmarried and very young.

Mary and Joseph journeyed from Nazareth to Bethlehem just before Jesus' birth, apparently alone (Luke 2:4-5). Jesus was born in either a stable or cave,[24] prompting the question of who would have been available to attend the birth.

Jesus' parents fled to Egypt to avoid Herod's massacre of male babies under the age of two (Matthew 2:13-15).

On the cusp of his public ministry Jesus was sent into the desert for forty days. He ate nothing during that time and then faced temptation on several levels (Matthew 4:1-11, Luke 4:1-13). While physically vulnerable, he faced tests of his spiritual strength. He was tempted to question God's care and provision, tempted to worship someone other than God, and tempted to test God.[25]

Throughout his ministry Jesus' teaching and actions left him vulnerable to criticism by the religious leaders. Jesus seemed to pursue vulnerability as he healed on the Sabbath, socialized with "sinners," and challenged the hypocrisy of religious leaders.[26] He showed his followers that in God's kingdom typical sources of influence, including religious rules, ethnic tribalism (Matthew 15:21-28), and political power (John 18:33-37) are not as powerful as the vulnerability of love. When he faced the people sent to arrest him for his provocative actions, Jesus rebuked Peter for using his sword to try to stop it from happening (John 18:10-11), rejecting violence and accepting the vulnerability of arrest and the events that followed.

At every pivotal moment from the time of his arrest to his final cry from the cross, Jesus embraced the vulnerable path in his response to events. When questioned by the most powerful religious and political leaders, Jesus' statements about his teaching and authority confirmed their fears and resulted in the sentence of crucifixion. Jesus never denied or obfuscated; he submitted to a process he could have stopped at any time.

The vulnerability of interrogation by the most powerful religious and political leaders paled in comparison to the vulnerability of crucifixion. Jesus was stripped, mocked, spit on and beaten before the public walk to Golgotha (Matthew 27:28-31). Having returned his clothing for that journey, the soldiers once again stripped him before crucifying him. One commentator notes, "To be stripped of clothing signified gross indignity and the loss of personal identity."[27] As Jesus hung on the cross witnesses hurled insults (Matthew 27:39-44). Finally, the cry recorded by Matthew and Mark, "My God, my God, why have you forsaken me?" reveals the most vulnerable aspect of the ordeal – feeling abandoned by God (Matthew 27:46; Mark 15:34).

In submitting to the crucifixion, Jesus embraced the vulnerability of physical pain, public humiliation, and the loss of his most intimate relationship.

The cross became the focal point for followers of Jesus because it demonstrates the limitless love of God. We meditate on the cross to renew our confidence in God's love. It can also renew our confidence in the power of vulnerability. The cross shows the lengths to which God will go to restore the relationship broken by sin. It also redeems vulnerability – reclaiming the power of vulnerability as a key element of the kind of relationships for which we were created. Rather than responding to vulnerability in ways that provoke shame, rather than responding from our fear, we can follow Jesus' example by responding in a way that brings healing.

We have the vision. God's vision is for loving relationships where it is safe to be vulnerable and to show others the truth of what we are experiencing, knowing we will be met with grace. The Christian community must be motivated by love, not fear, in order to be marked by the kind of relationships Jesus cultivated. We must be able to embrace vulnerability, to see it as central to our humanity. That requires connecting with our own fear and shame so that we can be present for others in their times of vulnerability. All of us experience both fear and shame. They are powerful emotions that provoke a wide range of reactions. They are so central to our experience of life that they shape the fundamental way we interact with God, others *and* ourselves. Because they are such important emotions, they *will* impact our relationships.

How, then, do we "connect" with fear and shame?

From the perspective of the IFS model, emotions like fear and shame are not just free floating, transient phenomena.[28] Our internal family members hold beliefs, emotions, images, and sensations. Because emotions like fear and shame are held by our internal family members, they are signals from them that they need our attention. They provide information about where we need healing. Just as we can turn to any person with compassion, as the leader of the inner family we can turn to the members of our inner family to provide the resources they need for healing.

While some members of our inner family need healing, others are like facets of a gemstone, bringing their qualities to enrich the family as a whole. From birth, we have an inner family whose members bring richness to our life. Ideally, there is a harmonious blend of different talents and qualities in the inner family, all working together under the leader of the family to support each individual's calling and purpose.

Sometimes we will experience this ideal sense of harmony. At other times, especially when circumstances are more distressing, we will feel some degree of chaos or rigidity inside. It became clear to Dr. Schwartz that some members of the family are primarily driven by fear and others are burdened by painful emotions such as shame and beliefs of unworthiness.[29] Most astonishing to him was that establishing relationships with these different family members allowed clients to access qualities that were universally present, no matter what the client had experienced in life.[30] Connection was the key to unleashing resources such as compassion, clarity, calm, and curiosity. As clients learned to differentiate themselves as leader of the family, they could draw on their intrinsic resources, turning *toward* their fearful internal family members to learn more about how those members were trying to protect them. This helped them be with the hurting members of their internal family to relieve their pain.

Consider the parallels between Dr. Schwartz's discoveries and the vision Jesus gave us for relationships. Jesus promised his followers that he would remain with them through the Counselor, the Holy Spirit, who would be with them forever (John 14:16). We are to "live by the Spirit," exhibiting the qualities of love, peace, patience, and gentleness that reflect a life led by the Spirit (Galatians 5:16,22). We are also created in God's image (Genesis 1:26-27). When we lead our inner family by drawing on the harmonious blend of the Spirit and the resources we possess as image-bearers we can fulfill the vision for relationships – to love God and one another as we love ourselves.

We have seen that fear of vulnerability can block those resources; fear can result in reactions to vulnerability such as judgment, rigidity, avoidance, oversimplification, and invalidating remarks. We react this way to others, and we react this way to ourselves. Fear breaks relationship, but love is the antidote to fear. Love dispels fear through relationship. God's presence provides the balm for our fear; when we lovingly turn toward our fear, we can connect with it. Dr. Schwartz discovered that fear is not the enemy; it is present for a reason.[31] It deserves our attention; the parts holding the fear need connection. Jesus turned toward anyone seeking his attention.[32] When we turn our attention inside with curiosity, we can connect with the parts of us who hold fear, build trusting relationships, and learn more about how they are trying to help. When those relationships are solid, we are also able to meet the most vulnerable members of our inner family, members who have been exiled to the margins of our consciousness because we fear what they hold.

When we are led by fear we treat our vulnerability much the same way Pharisees treated sinners, fearing sinners would pollute their purity and righteousness. When the Pharisees complained that Jesus kept company with sinners, he told them the parables of the lost, teaching them that each and every person is precious, and that he longs for their salvation (Luke 15:1-32). Salvation is a process, not an event; it is the process of transformation, of healing, and it is rooted in relationship. Again, following Jesus, we seek the exiled, the lost, the marginalized members of our inner family. As they are relieved of burdens such as painful emotions, distorted beliefs about their worth, and overwhelming images and sensations from traumatic experiences, they are free to contribute their life-giving qualities, reflecting God's image.

The fear and pain we hold inside limit the degree to which we can be present with an open heart when someone is struggling, and they limit our ability to draw close to God for comfort. They block the very resources we need most in times of difficulty. Cultivating a new spiritual practice of inner awareness and relationship gradually opens more space for grace, for ourselves and others. It enables us to reestablish leadership of our inner family, relying on the resources we have as image-bearers filled with the Spirit. It restores the loving relationships with God, ourselves, and one another for which we were created.

Before we delve more deeply into this practice, we need to examine how life experiences impact our development so we can better understand and embrace our vulnerability. Turning toward vulnerability is typically something we resist. The desire to avoid vulnerability is deeply rooted. Yet, as humans born into a fallen world, we simply cannot escape some degree of vulnerability, and, therefore, the fear that provokes strategies to avoid it. This is the fear that leads to the problematic responses to distress we have just reviewed. In order to fully appreciate how vulnerable we are, we now turn our attention to the developing brain.

Part Two
UNDERSTANDING OURSELVES

Chapter Six
BRAIN BASICS

Human brains develop primarily *after* birth. "The explosion in growth outside the womb gives us a far higher potential for learning and adaptability."[33] However, the fact that our brain is shaped by experience also makes us vulnerable to adversity. The brain is an incredibly complex organ, but a greatly simplified overview is sufficient to provide the most important information for our focus. I encourage you to pay special attention to the way experience shapes every aspect of our brain and mind.

Brain Structure

The basic building block of our brain is the *neuron*, a specialized cell in the nervous system that connects with other neurons to form the networks that allow our brain to function. We have over 100 billion neurons, each of which has an average of ten thousand connections to other neurons. Scientists believe we have about one *million billion* neural connections, making the brain the most complex structure, natural or artificial, on earth.[34] It's truly a magnificent organ! Both genes and early experience influence the way neurons connect to one another.

Structurally, the brain can be divided into three primary components.[35] The *lower brain*, primarily consisting of the *brainstem*, regulates basic bodily functions such as breathing, digestion, heart rate, temperature, the immune system, and the flow of energy through our body.[36]

The mid brain or *limbic system* has several important roles and structures. It is the "seat of the emotions, the monitor of danger, the judge of what is pleasurable or scary, the arbiter of what is or is not important for survival purposes. It is also a central command post for coping with the challenges of living within our complex social networks."[37] In other words, there is a lot going on in the limbic system – all of which impacts how we function in relationships.

The appraisal of meaning, the processing of social signals, and the activation of emotion all take place in the limbic structures.[38] The limbic system is very primitive at birth and is shaped by experience as experience influences both genes and temperament.[39] It includes the *hippocampus*, a key structure for memory, and the *hypothalamus* which links the body to the brain through hormones. Another component, the *amygdala*, is important for processing emotions, particularly fear, anger and sadness.[40] The amygdala is involved in appraising the meaning of incoming stimuli such as what we see, hear and feel.[41] As a result, the amygdala is essential to our social relationships. It is involved in the perception of facial expressions and regulation of our emotional states. It facilitates our understanding of the internal states of others, enabling us to attune to one another. As highly social creatures, we are constantly taking in information about the people around us, assessing the messages we receive – both verbal and non-verbal – to determine whether we are safe.

The brainstem and limbic system together form what we can think of as the "emotional brain."[42] This part of our brain operates *outside* of conscious awareness and alerts us to something important – whether dangerous or appealing – by releasing hormones. These hormones have a visceral impact ranging from mild queasiness to intense pressure in the chest associated with panic, getting our attention and shifting focus in a new direction. They govern heart rate, blood pressure, and respiration, preparing our body to respond to a threat.[43] This portion of the brain draws conclusions from general similarities, setting off physiological reactions *before* we can think or plan. "The detection of a person [or situation] as safe or dangerous triggers neurobiologically determined pro-social or defensive behaviors. Even though we may not always be aware of danger on a cognitive level, on a neurophysiological level, our body has already started a sequence of neural processes that would facilitate adaptive defense behaviors such as fight, flight, or freeze."[44]

Sally's experience illustrates this process. I was surprised to get a call from her. We worked together when she was grieving the loss of her mother and I hadn't seen her in a few years. She told me she'd had a panic attack while traveling and wanted to come in to explore what might have prompted it. She reported she and her husband were on a trip to the Wine Country in Napa and Sonoma, a very relaxing and enjoyable trip. They were touring a winery and she began to feel hot and sweaty, her heart rate rose, and she felt her chest constrict. She thought, "I'm going to die!" and was desperate to get outside. Sally was baffled by the panic attack, the first she'd ever experienced. Coming in the midst of a pleasurable trip, it seemed so "random." But it turned out not to be. In the cellar of the winery, the ceiling was low, the light was dim, and the stone walls were narrow. Revisiting that episode allowed Sally to connect with a memory from over 60 years earlier. As a young child she went to visit her older sister at the hospital. Her sister had polio and was in an iron lung. Sally looked through a small window in the door to her sister's room – then through a small window on the iron lung – and saw her sister lying in the metal tube. To her young eyes, it didn't look like her sister could breathe; it was terrifying. Entering the constricting environment of the wine cellar felt like entering the iron lung, and Sally's limbic system registered a major threat. In a matter of seconds, a memory she hadn't thought of in many, many years had her nervous system on high alert. She was not conscious of the early memory, but her limbic system was. The emotional brain plays an important role in monitoring safety. Thankfully, we also have another part of our brain that can help regulate responses to our environment.

The third part of the brain is the *neocortex*.[45] The bulk of the neocortex is comprised of the *frontal lobes*, which begin to develop rapidly in the second year of life.[46] This is the part of the brain that enables us to have abstract thoughts and complex reasoning, to reflect on our experience, to plan and communicate using language. The frontal lobes also enable us to feel empathy, which is our capacity to identify with the feelings, thoughts or attitudes of another person. The *mirror neurons* contained in our frontal lobes play a role in empathy, making us vulnerable to feeling both the positive and negative moods of others.[47] Empathy is currently believed to be the first step toward compassion, the feeling that prompts us to take action on another's behalf.[48]

It would make sense to think of the neocortex as "the boss," but it turns out that this region is highly influenced by the emotional brain – the limbic system and brainstem. Surprisingly, it's more of a *bottom up* than a *top down* process. "The more intense the visceral, sensory input from the emotional brain, the less capacity the rational brain has to put a damper on it."[49] We are constantly taking in information from our surroundings that registers in our emotional brain. When our emotional brain signals safety, the capabilities of our neocortex enable us to observe what is going on, predict the outcome of action, and make a choice.[50] Bringing this capacity for observation to our emotions, sensations, and thoughts, a capacity often referred to as *mindfulness*, is critical for maintaining healthy relationships. When the intensity of the input from the emotional brain overrides our capacity for mindfulness we become much more reactive and impulsive. Our response to situations can seem highly disproportionate, such as feeling rage in response to a minor slight. The intensity of our emotional response reflects the influence of memories.

Memory

Memory is more than just what we can consciously recall from past events. From the beginning of life memories are formed whenever the brain responds to experience and creates new neural networks.[51] Experiences continue to shape the brain throughout our life by altering the connections between neurons, creating new neural networks and new associations between those networks.[52] Perhaps you have heard the phrase, "What fires together wires together."[53] The more a particular neural network is activated, or "fires," the more likely it will be activated in the future. "Our perceptions are *based* on our neuronal firing pattern."[54]

Don had a dilemma. A strategy that was very helpful in some areas of his life, one that felt central to his identity, was causing problems in his marriage. As far back as he could remember, Don made every effort to anticipate how people would respond to him. He adjusted his posture, crafted his sentences, modulated his tone, and monitored his choices to minimize the potential for disappointing someone and maximize the likelihood that he would please others. His internal monitor, a protective part of his inner family, was always on duty, making it very difficult for Don to be fully present in the moment and hindering his ability to express his own desires. The monitoring felt essential despite the cost. And, paradoxically, the very activity he hoped would prevent others from being disappointed with him was frustrating for his wife. She experienced him as distant, preoccupied, disconnected and even mechanical. He was aware of his behavior but felt powerless to make any changes. "It's who I am," he said.

Don had an entrenched behavior reflecting a neural network that had been activated over and over. This type of neural network reflects the influence of experiences held as memories. There are two primary ways connections are made in the brain, resulting in the two forms of memory: *implicit* and *explicit*.[55] Implicit memory is a form of early, nonverbal memory present at birth – and perhaps before birth – that continues throughout life. Implicit memories hold emotions, behaviors, perceptions, and body sensations. Implicit memory involves parts of the brain that do not require conscious processing when memories are either encoded or retrieved.[56] We are not consciously aware when these memories are formed, or when they influence our present experience.

Repeated experiences are summarized and generalized by the brain and held in implicit memory as *mental models* that help us interpret present experiences and anticipate future ones.[57] These mental models help us more rapidly assess situations and respond to them. As a result, our response to present situations is influenced by these mental models, and our perception is biased by them. The influence of mental models occurs outside of our conscious awareness.

Some of our most important and influential mental models hold the experiences with our primary caregivers. The degree to which caregivers are responsive, attuned, predictable, perceptive, nurturing, and sensitive shape an individual's expectations for future relationships. For example, a young child whose mother consistently consoles and comforts her during times of distress will generalize that experience so that her mother's presence brings a sense of safety and security. In contrast, a young child whose mother consistently reacts to his distress with a tone of voice and facial expressions that are not comforting and soothing will generalize those experiences so that her presence evokes anxiety or confusion. The mental models of our primary caregivers are encoded in the brain by the first birthday.[58] These early mental models are held in implicit memory and continue to impact our experience of others. "Each of us filters our interactions with others through the lenses of mental models created from patterns of experience in the past."[59] Again, this is happening outside of our awareness, prompting automatic behaviors and reactions unless we intentionally explore and resolve the influence of early experiences on our functioning.

Explicit memory begins to form in the second year of life. We are aware that we are remembering explicit memories, which can be either factual or autobiographical.[60] Forming these memories requires focus – conscious, directed attention. We convey explicit memories when we tell stories, describe an experience, or relate a sequence of events.[61] Interestingly, recollections typically involve association of both explicit and implicit memories; our implicit memories cast a shadow on what we share verbally, as well as what we convey through nonverbal aspects of communication and behavior.[62]

We do not remember everything we experience. It is much more efficient for our brain to store things that are essential and to let go of things that are not. Experiences with little emotional intensity do not arouse our focus. Therefore, they register as less important and are not easily recalled later on.[63] Events with a "moderate to high degree of emotional intensity seem to get labeled as 'important' and are more easily remembered in the future."[64] We remember painful things such as insults and shaming most vividly because of the adrenaline we secrete to defend against a potential threat.[65] Emotions enhance the creation of new connections among our neurons, which also helps explain why we are more likely to remember something with a higher degree of emotional intensity.

Nothing carries more emotional intensity than a threat to our survival. Because we are born with such immature brains, we are highly dependent on our primary caregivers for survival. Our earliest experiences with caregivers fundamentally shape our future relationships, and the degree to which we fear vulnerability.

Chapter Seven
A TALE OF THREE BABIES

Noticing the early signs that her daughter was hungry, seeing the tiny tongue licking her lips and the little fist making its way to her daughter's mouth, Leah knew it was time to feed her again. She had done her research and knew that crying was a relatively late sign babies use to signal hunger. Over and over again, as frequently as less than an hour apart and sometimes, mercifully, three hours apart, her new baby showed those signs and Leah responded promptly to her need. When she was sleeping Leah left her in peace, consistently allowing her baby to signal when she needed comfort or food and when she was fine alone. What a beautiful interaction – the attuned mother watching her new baby and responding appropriately to her needs, creating the security that would help her daughter thrive.

Jill did not have that kind of mother. When she cried, she was often ignored. Sometimes her mother responded, but there was a disconnect; her mother did not recognize what she needed. Rather than watching her child with a caring gaze, her mother looked distracted and detached. When someone asked how she was adjusting to being a new mother, she responded with a brief, factual statement utterly lacking emotion. There were times when she knew what her daughter needed, but she dismissed the need. Over time, Jill learned to dismiss her own needs, aware that they would not be met.

Stacy never knew what to expect from her mother. Sometimes her needs were met in a sensitive and appropriate way, and sometimes they weren't. In fact, at times it seemed that her mother's needs compelled her mother's behavior. Stacy would be playing quietly and her mother would rush in with tickling, hugs and kisses that overwhelmed her and were distressing. Her mother didn't respond to her distress, leaving her confused and uncertain. She became preoccupied with her mother, watching closely to see if she would respond to her needs, never certain what to expect.

These three scenarios reflect the three most common outcomes of early childhood experiences with primary caregivers: secure attachment, avoidant attachment, and ambivalent attachment. Each child has the same basic needs, but parents differ in their response to those needs. Children have an "attachment system"[66] designed to seek proximity to caregivers so needs can be met. At the most basic level, this system is essential for survival because it fosters connection with the person who has the power to meet essential needs. These needs include physical protection, nourishment, and emotional connection. Because these are basic survival needs, the innate attachment system is highly sensitive to signs of danger. If needs are not met a child feels fear and anxiety. However, when a parent is responsive to a child's signals – signals that tell the parent the child wants to be close in order to have their needs met – the child senses safety and feels secure.

Ideally, a parent will be alert to the child's signals and will respond in a manner that is consistent with the child's needs. When this happens, the minor distress that prompted the infant to seek connection will be soothed, creating safety for the infant. Repeated experiences of attuned connection become part of implicit memory as mental models, creating the expectation for the infant that their needs will be met.

One of our primary and deepest needs is to be *known* – to be seen and accepted exactly as we are. In Jesus' interactions with people, we repeatedly see that he knew them individually. When Jesus arrived at the well at a town in Samaria he sat down and waited for a woman to come, a woman he knew needed to draw life from a trustworthy source (John 4:5-26). When Nicodemus approached Jesus with questions, Jesus took time to provide the detailed answers he needed (John 3:1-21). And when Zacchaeus climbed a tree to get a look at the teacher he had been hearing about, Jesus knew he needed the full revelation of Jesus' mission (Luke 19:1-10). If we imagine ourselves being in those scenes, we can allow him to meet our own need to be seen, to be known, to receive love. Jesus knows everything about us and accepts us just as we are. He calls us by name, as he gently and lovingly called Mary by name as she grieved by his tomb (John 20:16). Jesus meets us in every vulnerable situation, tenderly loving us in the specific way we need love. Parents provide this kind of love each time they respond in an attuned way to their infant's needs.

This important early relationship with the primary caregiver helps the child develop the capacity for self-regulation. The adult's internal state aligns with the child's when the child seeks attachment and the adult responds appropriately. It is a sort of dance – a movement of the child toward the parent and a corresponding response from the parent that is aligned with the child's needs. The child internalizes the parent's response, enabling the child to develop their own capacity for emotional regulation.

Parents bring their behavior, individual expectations, and early attachment experiences to the relationship with the child (who is born with a certain temperament). In addition, the relationship with the parent and child happens in the family and broader cultural context. Clearly, many variables contribute to the nature of the interaction between parent and child. The child adapts to the reality of the relationship, whether or not the primary caregiver responds in an attuned fashion. "Infants become attached to their caregivers whether or not those caregivers are sensitive and responsive."[67] Research shows that the earliest attachments are typically formed by the age of seven months, and these key attachments are formed with only a few important people.[68] A child can have a different kind of attachment to each primary caregiver because the nature of the attachment depends upon the adult's response to the child's needs.

Despite the fact that many variables contribute to the nature of the attachment between the parent and child, the most common outcomes fall into three categories: *secure*, *avoidant* and *ambivalent*.

Secure Attachment

When parents are consistently "emotionally available, perceptive, and responsive to their infant's needs and mental states,"[69] the infant will develop a secure attachment. The parent must accurately "perceive the internal world of the infant, make sense of it, and respond in a timely and effective manner."[70] No parent will be perfect in their attunement to their child. Therefore, repair is an important aspect of attunement.[71] When there's a rupture in the relationship, when the parent does not respond in a way that meets the child's needs, ideally there is a repair. Repairs reflect a flexible approach that is a consistent feature of secure attachment. For example, a mother might realize that her infant prefers bouncing rather than rocking when she's fussy. The rocking does not relieve distress but bouncing does. The infant does not get her need met initially, but the attuned parent persists until she is successful in meeting the child's needs. In this scenario, the child is learning that they have the capacity to impact both how they feel and how others respond.[72] Secure attachment is the outcome of "good enough" attunement where the child's needs are consistently met.

Avoidant Attachment

In Jill's case, her mother was consistently emotionally unavailable – disconnected, withdrawn, and distracted – and, therefore, unresponsive to her needs. At other times, her mother rejected her needs. When her mother did recognize a need, she was not effective at meeting it. This resulted in a different type of dance. Rather than a smoothly flowing, attuned signal and response, the emotional distance and rejecting response of Jill's mother resulted in avoidance on Jill's part. Rather than continuing to seek proximity in order for her needs to be met, Jill adapted by minimizing her efforts to connect with her mother. This is an instinctive response by the infant. It is not conscious. The experiences the infant has form the mental model that becomes the basis for the infant's expectations. Because it is essential for survival, the infant will adapt to the signals the parent sends. In Jill's case, that meant learning to minimize her needs. Unfortunately, this type of experience also results in a child believing something is wrong with her. It is not just wrong to need something; she is flawed because she has needs. These beliefs form later in the child's development but are based on these early experiences.

Ambivalent Attachment

Stacy had a different experience. Her mother was inconsistent in her responses. Rather than being in sync with Stacy's inner experience, her mother was sometimes intrusive. Stacy's mother was not reliably available, perceptive, or responsive because her own state of mind interfered with her ability to perceive her daughter's needs. As a result, Stacy was anxious and preoccupied with her distress, uncertain about whether her mother would meet her needs and not necessarily soothed by connection with her. Stacy's uncertainty about whether her needs would be met resulted in an anxious focus on her mother.[73] She adapted with a survival strategy: she took responsibility for monitoring whether her mother would meet her needs. Stacy would also believe that there is something wrong with her. In her case, the belief would likely be something like, "Am I lovable?" or "Am I worthy of love?" There is a lingering, anxious preoccupation with the other in important relationships.

It is important to remember that the infant's perception of their key attachment figures and the adaptations they make to them happen on an instinctive level. Infants are able to assess the quality of the attachment with their primary caregivers – by monitoring facial expression, posture, tone of voice, and movement – and adapt accordingly.[74]

These different attachment experiences are stored in implicit memory. They shape behavior, emotional regulation, and social relationships as the child develops.[75] The nature of our attachment to our primary caregivers has a powerful impact on how we function in the world. Often it is a key contributing factor to the difficulties adults experience that prompt them to seek help.

For example, as an adult Jill's early adaptive response leads her to dismiss the importance of emotional relationship with others, as well as her own emotional experience. She places a high value on independence, views her analytical and logical qualities as superior to emotional experience, and has a limited understanding of the influence of interpersonal relationships, minimizing any dependence on others.[76] She is mystified when her husband expresses frustration or sadness over the fact that their relationship feels more like a business partnership or compatible roommates. She is satisfied with their relationship and does not understand why he is not. In exploring her early childhood, she is quick to dismiss any emotional response on her part as exaggerated. She minimizes any distress associated with childhood memories, saying she had everything she needed – food, shelter, education, etc. There is no mention of emotional connection with her parents or other family members. She just does not understand why her husband feels something is lacking in their relationship.

In contrast to Jill, Stacy is often flooded with emotion from issues in her past. She is preoccupied with the quality of her relationships, longing for closeness and fearing losing it. She wonders whether important people really love her or whether they will abandon her. Past relationship experiences intrude on present relationships, making it difficult to perceive current situations accurately. When she repeatedly asks her boyfriend for assurance that he cares for her, he becomes frustrated that no matter what he does it does not seem to convince her that he is committed to the relationship. Stacy's desperate desire to connect becomes a barrier to the relationship she longs to achieve.[77]

The securely attached adult is able to live more fully in the present, neither denying the influence of key relationships in the past nor preoccupied with past and future relationship concerns. They are able to enjoy and regulate emotional intensity, which facilitates satisfying emotional connections with others. The story they tell about their past is rich with detail and reflects an understanding of the impact of early experiences, but those experiences do not typically intrude on the present.[78] Relationships tend to be both more fulfilling and more stable. Not to say that there aren't any challenges! Securely attached individuals will be more flexible in the face of challenges and better able to cope with the emotional impact of difficult experiences.

These three different styles of attachment are the most common dominant types. There is a fourth type of attachment, called *disorganized attachment*, that occurs when a parent or caregiver is either a source of abuse, or are themselves so preoccupied with their own trauma or other significant issues such as mental illness that they are unavailable to meet the child's needs. These children are caught in a terrible dilemma: the person who is necessary to their survival is also a source of distress or even terror.[79] The child's dilemma is evident in their behavior. When reunited with a parent after being separated the child might begin to approach then back away, or can even freeze and rock with an averted gaze.[80] Children with disorganized attachment do not have a caregiver who is reliably available to help them with emotional regulation, so they do not develop that capacity, impacting their sense of safety and ability to trust. Unfortunately, the inability to regulate emotional responses results in a tendency toward dissociation (disconnecting from reality), disruptive behavior, impairment of cognition and coping capacities, and even a vulnerability to Posttraumatic Stress Disorder (PTSD).[81] Other studies show that in young adults, disorganized attachment can lead to destructive impulsivity, intense anger, and chronic suicidal behavior.[82]

The effects of disorganized attachment dramatically illustrate infants' dependence on their primary caregivers to meet fundamental emotional, not just physical, needs. In fact, when an infant expresses a physical need, such as the need for food, they are also expressing the emotional need for closeness, comfort, and responsiveness. The need for connection, and the degree to which it is met, play a significant role in our development and our ongoing sense of wellbeing. Whether the outcome of our early attachment experiences is secure, avoidant, ambivalent, or disorganized, the need for attuned connection persists.

The types of attachment we have explored in this chapter reflect the nature of communication between the caregiver and infant. Ideal communication, communication where the person receiving the message responds to what was actually communicated, fosters relationship. The response babies receive from their caregivers creates their sense of self. When they experience attuned communication, they feel understood, their need is validated, and they know they are not alone in the world.[83] This core way of experiencing connection is vital to a child's sense of wellbeing, and when this need is not met, they often experience intense emotion. The more intense the emotion, the greater the need for attuned connection, and the more vulnerable the child is to an insensitive response from a caregiver.[84] The need for this kind of attuned communication is central to our relationship with God, others, and ourselves throughout life. Exploring the importance of attuning to our own and others' emotional experience is the next step in more fully understanding ourselves.

Chapter Eight
The Heart of the Matter

While reading each of the following vignettes, bring your awareness to your body and mind. Notice if you resonate with any of the situations, or if you find yourself distancing from some of them. Scan your body to see if you feel any sensations and notice if thoughts arise. You might see images of your own experiences of similar emotions. By entering into these scenes and sharing the emotions felt by each of these people, we connect with them. It is by sharing emotions that we connect with one another.[85] And connection is our most fundamental need.

****

I close my eyes and bring her to mind. The velvety skin, the glossy curls, the deep blue eyes…and that smile! She smiles at me with her whole body as though she can't contain her joy. It fills me with joy I, too, can't contain. I feel it in my face, my heart, my limbs. I want to hold her and hug her and dance. *This* is the joy my friends who are grandparents have been telling me about. It is as pure and radiant and incredible as they promised it would be.

****

Sitting at the kitchen table, she thinks about leaving the house. She knows she feels better when she can take a walk or run an errand. They could really use some things from Costco. Then she sees herself walking into that huge store. There are men everywhere. She is sure they are looking at her. The fear that started as a twinge is now filling her torso and closing her throat. Memories of the day she was assaulted start flashing through her mind. She can't catch her breath. Tears fill her eyes as she stares at the front door, knowing today will not be a day when she is able to leave the house.

****

It was consuming him. There was no space for anything else. No other thoughts, no other actions, no other feelings. The rage was like a caged animal, pacing and roaring and ready to pounce if the door opened even slightly. His heart raced, he was sweating, all of his muscles were tense, he could not sit still. He thought of all of the ways he could hurt the person who chose to get in a car and drive after drinking – the person who killed his son.

****

It's a perfect day to head to the summit. The powder is fresh and light and the sky is crystal clear. There's no wind and the air is just crisp enough to be invigorating. He feels a little tingle of excitement as he exits the lift. The slope drops off quickly, and as he stands at the top evaluating the best route down, the excitement builds. His heart rate speeds up just enough and he knows it's time to commit. The speed is exhilarating! Being on the fine edge of fast but not out-of-control keeps him intensely focused as he makes choices about navigating the terrain. After a hard stop with a big rooster tail of snow he's gliding over to ride the chair, enjoying the last of the adrenaline rush before doing it all again.

****

Eight years ago? How could it be? She would have been 13 today. She tidies the gravestone and places fresh flowers by it. Tears flow as she tells her little girl how much she misses her. The pain still crushes her heart. Her whole body feels limp as she lets the sadness wash over her. The emptiness she feels as she longs to hold her daughter in her arms drags her down into a swirling vortex that threatens to pull her under. Her son touches her shoulder. She clutches his hand, and the wave begins to pass.

****

To experience deeper relationship with God, one another, and ourselves, we need to regain our emotional competence. Emotional competence requires awareness of our own emotions, the ability to effectively share our emotions with others, and the capacity for empathic understanding of others' emotions.[86] I say "regain" because, to differing degrees, all of us have experiences in relationships that affect our emotional competence.

Emotion in the broadest sense is a process, not just the individual feelings evoked by the different vignettes above. The process of an *emotional response* begins when the brain and various systems in the body orient to a stimulus of some kind. This initial "orienting response" happens because there is awareness – whether conscious or unconscious – that something important is happening.[87] Following this awareness is the assessment of whether what is happening is "good" or "bad" – whether one should "approach" or "withdraw."[88] The physiological arousal of an emotional response tells us, "I want more of this" or "I want less of this."[89] The meaning attached to the stimulus results in a flow of energy in our system associated with *categorical* emotions such as fear, anger, joy, or sadness. We then reveal these internal emotional states through nonverbal signals such as tone of voice, facial expressions, and movement in our body.[90] At this point our internal emotional experience becomes a form of communication with others. When others perceive and respond to our emotional signals we feel connected; we feel known and understood.

Effective communication of our emotional state can be disrupted in two fundamental ways that exist at opposite ends of a continuum. On one end lies repression, a state where we disconnect from our emotions and, therefore, lack the connection – both with ourselves and others – that freedom of emotional expression provides. On the other end lies chaos or dysregulation, a state where we lack control over our emotional expression. This state also inhibits connection because emotional outbursts or impulsive behaviors overwhelm others and impact their ability to be open to our experience.

Ideally, over the course of development we learn to be present to our emotions and to regulate the expression of emotion. When we can experience our own emotions without repression or chaos, we are able to fully connect with ourselves. Our relationship with ourselves facilitates the next element of emotional competence, where our innate empathy is available to enable us to connect with another person's emotional experience. Development of emotional competence occurs in relationship, beginning with the relationship with our primary caregivers.

Infants have no capacity to regulate their emotions.[91] Spend a few hours with an infant and you will see how quickly their emotional state shifts and how robustly they express their needs! Infants are dependent on their caregivers for regulation of their emotional states.[92] The caregiver's response to the child provides the regulation they need. Brain structures responsible for the experience and modulation of emotions develop in response to parental input.[93] The degree to which the caregiver is able to attune to the child's emotional cues and respond in a way that signals understanding of the child's needs impacts the degree to which the infant feels secure in the world. When a parent's response is attuned, the child's experience of herself is that she is "good."[94] Security and the confidence that one is loved and worthy of relationship provide the safe container for freedom of emotional experience. Because early experiences shape brain structures they are the template for future relationships with ourselves and others. "We will understand ourselves as we have felt understood, love ourselves as we perceived being loved on the deepest unconscious levels, [and] care for ourselves with as much compassion as…we perceived as young children."[95]

Whenever research shows the impact of parenting on a child's development there is a risk of placing blame on parents for their shortcomings. It is essential to realize that in the vast majority of cases parents and other primary caregivers are doing their best. They do not set out to invalidate their child's emotional experience, or to adversely impact their development of emotional competency. It bears repeating that many factors contribute to a parent's response to their child. All of us are the product of the generations that precede us. "Whatever affected one generation but has not been fully resolved will be passed on to the next."[96] We begin to see the fallacy of blame when we recognize that all parents carry the legacy of previous generations, which can include strategies that were adaptive at a certain point but no longer serve us well in current relationships. For example, many immigrants fled starvation, war, and persecution. Often, a stoic repression of emotion is a necessary survival strategy in those circumstances. The value placed on stoicism can lead a parent to dismiss or deny a child's emotional experience. The parent intends to teach the child something valuable, not realizing that they are sending a message a young child interprets as, "I'm bad for feeling sad (or angry or fearful…)." Without resolution, this child learns to repress their emotional experience, and is at risk as a parent of perpetuating that pattern.

Blame would be a dead-end for both parents and children. If instead the focus is on responsibility, on the need to learn to connect with ourselves so we can better connect with others, then we have a path forward to break patterns that inhibit emotional competence. With the caution about blame in the forefront of our minds, we can delve more deeply into the way children respond to messages about their emotional experience.

Emotions are a young child's only form of communication. If a child expresses sadness or anger and no one is there to provide comfort or containment, there is a sense of isolation and danger that is highly anxiety-provoking. It is imperative for children to learn how to get their basic needs for connection and protection met, so they will adapt to their parent's response. For example, if a parent is overwhelmed by their own stress – which can reflect myriad issues such as financial difficulties, mental or physical health issues, problems in the extended family, etc. – the child will realize on an instinctive, subconscious level that his own emotional state is a burden that the parent cannot handle. He will learn to suppress his emotions, to be self-sufficient, not "needy."[97] If a parent is unresponsive, a child might adapt by escalating their demand for attention through crying, tantrums, or acting out.

If a child exists in an environment that consistently sends a message that her emotions are not welcome, she adapts by cutting off from them, losing the information that her emotions provide. It is not only difficult emotions such as fear, sadness and anger that provoke an invalidating response from caregivers. Even emotions such as joy and playfulness can be met with a response that they are unwelcome. The messiness and exuberance of a child's happiness can feel overwhelming to a parent due to stress, or their own experience of feeling shamed as a child for having similar emotions. Children will do what is required to adapt, losing connection with their own emotional experience and losing the ability to fully connect to others.

The spontaneous exuberance and joy of young children should be delightful. Ideally, we would want to join them, to meet them with the same unrestrained energy. It is the energy of *worship*. King David, rejoicing over the return of the ark to the City of David, danced "before the Lord with all his might" (2 Samuel 6:14). Children show us the energy God gave all of us to worship with abandon, to express our emotions without shame or hesitation. Losing this freedom is a costly outcome of an environment that invalidates or represses emotional expression.

It is not unusual for children to learn to repress their emotions. In addition to the impact of adaptations made by previous generations and the myriad stressors impacting parents, we also live in a culture that prioritizes thinking over feeling. Emotion is often relegated to a lesser status, as though emotions are more primitive and less valuable than our uniquely human capacity for reason and analysis and logic. It seems protective to assign a higher priority to reason when so many of us receive messages about our emotions being invalid. We can begin to reclaim the importance of emotion as essential to reason when we recall that emotion assigns value to things. Rather than seeing reason and emotion as separate phenomena occurring in different compartments of our brain, current neuroscience teaches us that both are elements of an integrated system. The ability to reason rests on the ability of our body to perceive our environment, on our emotions to inform and energize our response, and only then on our capacity for evaluation to make a decision.[98]

It might come as a surprise to learn that reason is informed by emotion. Most of us have learned the opposite; we have been taught that emotions interfere with reasoning. Clearly, there are times when intense emotions can cloud our judgment, but research has found that the opposite is equally true. Insufficient connection to our emotional experience "is an equally important source of irrational behavior."[99] Thus, the ability to connect to our emotion, and to connect to our bodies where our emotions manifest, is essential to doing our best thinking. And, it turns out, if we are going to err in one direction or the other, we should err on the side of attending to emotion. A prominent neuroscientist writes,

> I see feelings as having a truly privileged status…because of their inextricable ties to the body, they come first in development and retain a primacy that subtly pervades our mental life…And since what comes first constitutes a frame of reference for what comes after, feelings have a say on how the rest of the brain and cognition go about their business. Their influence is immense.[100]

It is evident that repressing our emotions will hinder our ability to connect with ourselves and others. What about the other end of the continuum where chaos reigns? Often, this end of the continuum reflects an environment where a child was exposed to adversity, our next topic.

Chapter Nine
LIVING LIFE WITH A DIFFERENT NERVOUS SYSTEM

During graduate school aspiring therapists spend a year in a clinical setting to begin to learn to translate theories into practice. About three months into my clinical training at a hospice I was starting to feel a bit more confident that I had something to offer my clients. That confidence flew out the window the day I met Sheila.

I felt some trepidation even before our first session because I knew from the brief notes provided by the hospice team that she was a young woman whose infant son died shortly after birth. I was very aware of my inexperience as I showed her to our consultation room, my heart pounding, hoping that I could offer her something that would help her through one of the most difficult losses anyone can experience. I will never be quite sure why, but during our first session Sheila not only shared about her son, she also disclosed a significant history of early childhood physical and sexual abuse, a story she told me she had never shared with anyone. Part of me was saying, "I have no idea how to help her with this!" Fear of doing harm kept me from saying much at all.

At the time I knew very little about the impact of childhood trauma, let alone how to treat it. It was clear that Sheila was tired of living with the impact of her childhood experiences, so I relied heavily on supervisors and research to provide as much help as possible. The burdens she carried had a profound impact on all aspects of her life, including her parenting and her marriage. When she was triggered, the intense emotions and flashbacks made it difficult for her to respond to what was happening in the present moment in an appropriate way. She sometimes felt rage, and she had a pervasive sense of worthlessness. She got little sleep because she spent the wee hours of the morning on the internet searching for ways to kill herself.

In my mind's eye I can still see the photos Sheila shared of her childhood. The little girl in the pigtails looked so vulnerable. How could a father go into her room at night and molest her? How could he beat her with a wooden paddle for the slightest infraction? The abuse she suffered was so intolerable she first attempted suicide when she was six years old. By the time I met her, when she was in her twenties, she had attempted suicide several other times and routinely engaged in self-harm. And yet, despite her daily struggles, I saw glimpses of the playful little girl when she would talk about her love for animals and show me her latest tattoo, which was always a character from a children's story. As I watched Sheila be fiercely protective of a daughter born with special needs, I also saw echoes of the little girl who had the strength and courage to take the wooden paddle and throw it away. Over the years that we worked together she would often tell me her responsibility for her daughter was the only thing keeping her alive. But I also saw other qualities that helped her survive – her humor and tenacity and hope. Those qualities helped her persevere through the difficult work of healing from her trauma. I saw that, despite the horrific abuse she suffered, she still possessed the resources she needed for healing.

Over the course of our time together, I realized what a gift Sheila had given me when she chose to share her story with me. Her struggles and her desire to heal inspired me to learn all that I could about the impact of trauma and the best ways to heal from it. I did not fully realize at the time that most of my clients would have adverse experiences that, while often not as severe as Sheila's, were at the root of the issues that brought them to therapy.

Adverse experiences resulting in lifelong mental and physical health consequences affect the *majority* of children. A landmark study was done in the late 1990's on a large population of over 17,000 patients enrolled in an HMO to research the effects of adverse childhood experiences (ACE's).[101] The researchers identified ten ACE's including emotional or physical abuse, sexual abuse, emotional neglect, physical neglect, separation or divorce, witnessing domestic violence, exposure to drug or alcohol abuse, a mentally ill caregiver, and incarceration of a family member. The results showed that ACE's are far more common than previously understood. More than two-thirds of respondents reported at least one ACE, and more than one in five reported three or more ACE's. Because study participants were "mostly white, middle class, middle aged, well-educated and financially secure enough to have good medical insurance"[102] this was not considered a high risk population. The study showed that the more ACE's a person reported, the more likely they were to have mental health issues, physical health issues, and family dysfunction.

One of the researchers who led the original ACE study said

it only identifies "the tip of the iceberg" in terms of the types of experiences that can impact wellbeing.[103] Researchers have found that exposure to other common challenges also impacts the developing brain.[104] The broader Childhood Trauma Questionnaire screens for issues such as death of an important caregiver, prolonged illness, and "major upheaval."[105] Major upheaval can include myriad stressors such as multiple moves, deployment of a parent, financial changes such as job loss or loss of a home, and bullying at school or online. The list is long, a reminder that all of us grow up in a world full of adversity that can have long-term consequences for our wellbeing.

We explored how our early experiences shape our sense of safety in the world. When those early years include either traumatic events or chronic dysfunction "the world is experienced with a different nervous system."[106] The individual is focused on "suppressing inner chaos" and has an "altered perception of risk and safety."[107] As a result, a survivor of trauma has difficulty determining whether a situation is dangerous or safe. This impacts their relationships because the most basic assessment we make in relationships is whether the other person is safe and, therefore, trustworthy, or not. Misreading situations can lead to misunderstandings, resulting in conflict or cutoff in response to another person's innocuous comments or even facial expressions.[108]

This heightened emotional reactivity reflects the impact of trauma on brain structures. For individuals with Posttraumatic Stress Disorder (PTSD), "the critical balance between the amygdala [the portion of the brain that detects a threat] and the medial prefrontal cortex [the portion of the brain that evaluates/reasons] shifts radically" making it "much harder to control emotions and impulses."[109] It is important to recognize that the reaction the traumatized person has is largely outside of their control, which causes significant distress. "Intense and barely controllable urges and emotions make people feel crazy – and makes them feel they don't belong to the human race…As a result, shame becomes the dominant emotion…"[110]

Shame is the emotion we feel when we believe we are defective, when we believe that the adverse experiences happened because of *who* we are, and that it was our fault. The beliefs that accompany shame, that result from the kinds of adversity studied by the researchers, include things like, "I am unlovable; I'm bad; I'm worthless." The younger we are when we experience adversity the more likely we are to internalize these beliefs about our own defectiveness, provoking shame. Because children are "at the center of their own universe," they are vulnerable to interpreting everything that happens to them from this egocentric perspective.[111] The child exposed to trauma expects maltreatment and, without help to resolve the impact of early adversity, continues to blame themselves for difficulties in relationships throughout life.

When we hear someone take the blame for something that happened to them, especially as a child, it is natural to try to talk them out of it. How could they take responsibility for something an adult did when they were so young? One trauma survivor helps us understand the impact of these well-intentioned but misinformed responses. "When you try to talk me into being more reasonable I only feel *even more lonely and isolated* – and it confirms the feeling that nobody in the whole world will ever understand what it feels like to be me."[112]

"Even more lonely and isolated." A person suffering the effects of trauma – whether the traumatic event(s) happened in childhood or later in life – often feels lonely and isolated. The shame provoked by beliefs about worthlessness and self-blame often keeps people silent. So when they do muster up the courage to share their story, when they crack open the door to the most vulnerable place inside of them, we need to know how to connect with them in that sacred space.

Part Three
A New Spiritual Practice

Chapter Ten
A WAY FORWARD

My sister and I were talking one day about a complex situation concerning a friend of hers. This friend was struggling with her teenage daughter, and I was doing my best to offer what I know about the types of things that underlie the symptoms she was describing. At one point my sister asked, with disbelief and concern, "Are we really that fragile?"

Perhaps you have asked yourself the same thing during our survey of the ways relationships impact our developing brains, and how early experiences shape the way we make meaning of the world and interact with those around us. It is difficult to accept how vulnerable we are. We simply do not arrive in this world without the possibility of being wounded. There is no escaping vulnerability. We will be wounded to some degree, often by the people we love the most.

If being vulnerable is a basic part of our humanity, why is it so frightening? During those early months and years when we are so dependent on caregivers for all of our needs, our experiences with vulnerability can leave us with burdens of intense emotions like shame, grief, and terror. When needs are not met there can be a sense of abandonment. Feeling alone when we are not yet able to take care of ourselves fills us with fear. At an early age we believe everything is our fault, so we often decide that bad things happen because we are unlovable and unworthy.

These wounds from early vulnerability to the influences of our environment often do not heal without intentional effort. Sometimes subsequent life experiences are sufficiently positive to allow these wounds to heal, but, most often, we find ways to cover over the wounds so we are protected from pain. Without healing, no matter how hard we try to protect ourselves, the wounds are still lurking under the protective layer, waiting to be exposed and rendering us vulnerable to pain once again.

We spend a lot of energy running from the vulnerability inside ourselves and the vulnerability that is all around us. The responses to distress that we surveyed in Part I are examples of strategies we use to protect ourselves from others' pain and the pain that their distress might reveal in us. When we engage in protective strategies we undermine what we most need when we are struggling – relationship. Meaningful relationship only happens when we have the courage to be vulnerable: courage to let someone see our true feelings, to know our true story, to share when we do not know how the other will respond. However, the very relationship we most need seems fraught with risk, so we armor up or hunker down and settle for far less than the loving relationships for which we were created.

Because our wounds provoke fear of vulnerability, the way forward requires healing. In order to connect lovingly with another person who is in distress we need to invest energy in our own healing journey. Otherwise we will continue to meet another person's distress with protective strategies designed to avoid our vulnerability, our own pain. We will distance ourselves, rely on pat answers, or even judge. The more we open ourselves to the Spirit's tender and gracious leading about our own wounds, the more we can support others in their healing.

When we practice the spiritual discipline of confession we examine our attitudes, behaviors, impulses, thoughts, and emotions – the whole gamut of our experience. This practice takes us inside of ourselves. When we turn our attention inside we recall such things as conversations, thoughts, and impulses to act in certain ways. We quickly identify ways that we fall short of Jesus' example – of the people God intends for us to be. Jesus often refers to the "heart" – what we might think of as the inner source of all that we do. "For the mouth speaks what the heart is full of" (Matthew 12:34). Confession is not meant to provoke shame or condemnation. God wants to heal our brokenness and examining our "heart," the inner landscape, helps us know what needs healing.

The journey of healing begins in our inner world because that is where we hold our wounds and our protective strategies, which ensure the distress of those experiences do not affect us in the present. Bringing awareness to the inner world might be a new practice for you; most of us are much more familiar with noticing things in the external world. Try shifting your attention inside for a moment.

What is the first thing you notice?

Some possibilities include:
- *A thought* – you remember something you need to tend to or you have a response to the idea of noticing your inner

experience.

- *An emotion* – you are aware of something like sadness, boredom, or irritation.
- *An image* – a person comes to mind, or you recall a recent experience, or even something from your past bubbles up to the surface.
- *A sensation* – maybe you are hungry or you have some tension in your shoulders or you feel some fatigue in your eyes.
- *An impulse* – you notice wanting to get up from your chair, wanting to move in some way.

When we bring attention to our inner world we will notice all of these things. If we keep our focus on whatever we notice first, we will often realize that a sensation is linked to an emotion, and that we get an image along with the sensation and emotion, and some thought or belief accompanies all of that. It soon seems as though there are many different people residing inside!

If this seems to be a stretch, hang in there with me to see if this feels true for you. While most of us have not consciously thought of ourselves this way, it is common to hear something like, "Part of me wants to quit my job, but another part of me really enjoys the challenge." We often have conflicting emotions or ideas – sometimes even many different responses to a person or situation simultaneously! The Apostle Paul lamented, "I do not understand what I do. For what I want to do I do not do, but what I hate I do" (Romans 7:15). Another version of this verse lays the conflict bare: "What I don't understand about myself is that I decide one way, but then I act another, doing things I absolutely despise" (Romans 7:15, The Message).

Part III – A New Spiritual Practice

Recall a time when you acted in a way that you realized is not consistent with your values. Did you find yourself thinking something like, "I'm a terrible person!"? Broadening our perspective allows us to see that this one action does not represent all of who we are. Widening our focus in this manner creates space for grace. When we have the thought, "I'm a terrible person," the perspective of grace helps us recognize, "A part of me just responded in a way that's not consistent with what I believe." We can readily see that there are differences between the part that acted in a certain way, another who judges the action, and still another who acts graciously and compassionately toward the one who stumbled.

The perspective that we are "multiple" – that we have a variety of parts, or subpersonalities, might not seem as surprising when we remember we are created in God's image. God exists in relationship – Father, Son, and Holy Spirit – or Source of Love, Revealer of Love, and Presence of Love. So it makes sense that we also notice different facets of ourselves when we begin paying closer attention. Our multiplicity differs from God's; while God is three co-equal persons, the analogy for our multiplicity is more like the relationship of Christ and the Church. Christ is the head of the Church that is called "his body" (Colossians 1:24). As with our human bodies, the body of the Church has diverse parts with different functions (1 Corinthians 12:14-20). "The body is a unit, though it is made up of many parts; and though all its parts are many, they form one body." Paul also cautions us against privileging some parts over others. "The eye cannot say to the hand, 'I don't need you!'...those parts of the body that seem to be weaker are indispensable, and the parts that we think are less honorable we treat with special honor." The analogy Paul uses for the Church also describes what we find when we turn our attention to our inner world.

In our inner family, there is a leader and there are parts that bring unique qualities and gifts. Rather than being a symptom of a mental disorder, as some fear when introduced to the concept, multiplicity is actually a reflection of God's exquisite design for humans. Most of us readily accept the idea that our personalities have different traits such as the degree of introversion or extroversion. The perspective that we have multiple parts within us just takes the concept of personality traits one step further. It is also consistent with the idea of a body with many different, valuable parts. The best analogy is to think of ourselves as having a family of different persons inside of us.

As in any well-functioning family, our inner family must have leadership. Consider the idea that leadership for our inner family comes from a place where we are in harmony with the Holy Spirit. The Spirit is given to us as our guide, our advocate, our Counselor.[113] The Spirit empowers us to "fix our eyes on Jesus" (Hebrews 12:2), who shows us the way to love. As beloved children created in God's image, we also have intrinsic resources that we can draw upon. These resources are such things as love, compassion, grace, mercy, courage, wisdom, and joy, to name a few. The harmonious blending of the Spirit's counsel with the resources we possess as God's image-bearers provides the leadership for our inner family.

While we share common resources as evidence of God's image in us, each of us is also unique. Our uniqueness comes from a rich blend of qualities, characteristics and spiritual gifts. In the family analogy we are using, these qualities are contributed by our "family members." In a high functioning "family" the diverse members all work together under loving leadership that is in harmony with the Holy Spirit.

If this is the goal, what is the reality? Many of us would describe our inner family as dysfunctional: recall Paul's lament, "For what I do is not the good I want to do…" When we turn our attention inside we often notice warring factions. There are fears and frustrations bumping up against compassion and mercy. At times we are overwhelmed by grief or anxiety to the point where those emotions seem to blot out all else. It feels like the leader has left the building. We maintain a semblance of calm and clarity for a time and then a threat registers – a spouse is distant, a child is troubled, a boss is critical – and we spiral into shame or anger or defensiveness. "For what I want to do I do not do…" We are exquisitely sensitive to threats, quickly losing our Spirit-led ability to respond in ways that reflect our values.

Given our sensitivity to threats and vulnerability, it is not surprising that our inner family includes a team of *protectors* dedicated to anticipating or responding to the risk of being wounded. It is their job to either *proactively* manage risk or *reactively* respond when danger erupts. Not only does our protective team want to avoid new wounds, it wants to keep the old wounds from being exposed. Wounds that we already carry are held by another group of family members – the *exiles*. These are the family members our protectors keep locked away – or exiled – because they hold the distorted beliefs, painful emotions, and distressing images from earlier experiences.

In many instances the protectors take charge. They take over the leadership role we are meant to have. They believe it is up to them to protect us, and either do not know us as leader, or do not trust us because they do not have a relationship with us. In order to effectively lead our inner family, to build loving relationships *inside* as the foundation for having loving relationships with God and others, we must begin with our protectors.

Chapter Eleven
BEFRIENDING OUR PROTECTORS

Charlie looked dejected. He was slumped on the couch in my office looking everywhere but at me. Initially, he enthusiastically shared plans for marketing his business; then his expression shifted and he looked despondent. I remarked that I noticed the shift in his posture and expression and asked what he was noticing inside. He said, "I am such a fraud. If I market my business everyone is going to figure that out. What an idiot I am to think that's a good idea! I don't know why I just spent all of that money developing a marketing plan."

Part of Charlie was excited about the opportunity to grow his business, but the vulnerability of being more exposed seemed intolerable to one of his protectors, so it stepped in to shut down the plan. We can think of this part of Charlie as a "risk manager." Most large businesses have a department with a team of people dedicated to proactively identifying and minimizing risks. We have a similar team inside of us, a team of managers who proactively assess our environment and work to block any activity or relationship that seems too risky. Often, one or more members of our managerial team use criticism as a strategy to protect us from vulnerability. Charlie's inner manager called him a "fraud" and an "idiot." Charlie also noticed that when his critical manager jumped in his neck and shoulders felt tight.

I asked Charlie if he was open to learning more about why the critical protector showed up after he shared about marketing his business. "Not really. What a downer! I really enjoy the creative process of developing marketing strategies and he just jumps in to shut things down." I said, "It sounds like the part of you that has fun developing the marketing plan is not a big fan of the manager who's criticizing you. I wonder whether he would be open to giving us some space so we can find out more about why the protector thought he needed to criticize you."

When we turn our attention to our inner family it is rare for just one family member to show up at a time. As with any external family, when one person speaks another often chimes in with a different perspective. Just as we cannot productively speak to multiple people simultaneously, when we turn our attention inside we need to connect with one family member at a time. Often, it is sufficient to simply ask one part of us if it is willing to step aside to let the other speak, just as we would ask members of any group to take turns talking.

We can imagine our inner family as the cast of a play. In this analogy, Charlie is the director. He invites one of the cast members to step into the spotlight at the center of the stage while the others wait in the wings. Not only can Charlie have a productive dialogue because he is speaking to only one person, the feelings and beliefs held by the other cast members do not influence Charlie. Charlie is not *blended* with the attitudes of the other characters. By having one cast member speak at a time, Charlie is able to *unblend* from the various cast members so he can function as the leader – the director. He can speak to the person with an open heart, from a place of curiosity. As leader of the inner family, when he is unblended from the other cast members he can draw upon the resources he possesses because he is made in God's image.

One of the surprising things we learn when we turn our attention inside is that what we thought were disconnected thoughts, emotions, images, and sensations are actually held by individual members of our inner family. As with any person, our inner family members cannot be reduced to a single emotion or behavior, so we do not refer to them as "the angry one" or the "critic." What we first encounter in connecting with our parts might be a dominant aspect of how they are currently operating. However, that reflects the job they feel they must do to protect us; it does not reflect their essence. You might think of it as a costume they don or a uniform they wear; it is something that can be discarded once the threat they are focused on is resolved. *Note that the family member itself is not discarded!* Each of our family members brings something valuable to our system. The journey of healing is a journey of transformation. As healing occurs, family members' roles transform from something done out of fear to something that contributes to the optimal functioning of the whole family.

After asking the "marketing consultant" to step aside, allowing Charlie to unblend from it, Charlie noticed that he felt curious about the critical manager. I encouraged him to see whether the manager would tell him more about how he was trying to help. It might seem paradoxical to assume that a part dominated by criticism wants to be helpful because they can say some pretty nasty things. However, one assumption we can confidently make is that our protectors always have a positive *intention*. Whatever strategy they employ the underlying desire is to help in some way.

When Charlie asked, he learned that the manager feared marketing his business would expose him to ridicule because people would learn that he could not perform as promised. Charlie was able to remain curious, so he asked where he got the idea that Charlie was not capable. A scene came to mind from early in elementary school. The little boy was participating in the school-wide spelling bee, having won the honor of the best speller in his class. When he was asked to spell a word in front of the whole school assembly he froze. It was not a difficult word, but he could not respond. He was overwhelmed with shame when children giggled, and the shame persisted when he saw that his teacher and parents were disappointed in him. After this memory surfaced, I prompted Charlie to ask the manager if he took on his job at that time. The manager said he decided at that moment he would never let something like that happen again.

The protectors we think of as the "risk managers" in our family system *proactively* identify situations that could expose vulnerabilities and try to avoid them. As soon as the "marketing consultant" in Charlie's inner family got going with his planning, the critical manager began lobbing insults to shut the whole plan down. The little boy held the shame and the belief that he was a failure, and the manager did not want these burdens to overwhelm Charlie again if he was not able to live up to the goals of the marketing plan.

What if the manager is unsuccessful in stopping the process?

Part III – A New Spiritual Practice

What happens if Charlie moves forward to implement his new marketing plan? It is possible Charlie would be so successful his critical manager would quiet down until the next threat surfaced. However, if Charlie made promises to potential clients that he could not fulfill, it is likely he would start feeling like he was failing. The painful emotions and beliefs held by the little boy could bubble up to the surface. When the feelings and beliefs stored from an original wound resurface, when the "risk managers" are not successful in proactively shutting down something that might make us vulnerable, another kind of protector jumps in. These protectors are our first responders; they come on the scene when the house is on fire and do whatever it takes to put the fire out. They are *reactive*, showing up after the dreaded feelings and beliefs surface and threaten to overwhelm us.

Just as firefighters do not hesitate to turn on the full force of the hose to put out the fire, regardless of the secondary damage the water might cause, our reactive firefighter family members have a single-minded purpose: to stop the pain. They are not concerned about the ancillary damage their strategy might cause. In Charlie's case, feelings of failure prompted him to drink too much. On days when he heard about dissatisfied clients he found himself longing for that first glass of scotch. Toward the end of the day, he had difficulty focusing on his work because he just wanted to be home having a drink, and maybe two or three drinks – whatever it took to forget those unpleasant phone calls. He did not think about the fact that his wife would be upset with him for drinking again or that he tended to have no patience for his children when he drank. He just wanted to stop ruminating about the unhappy clients. He wanted to stop feeling the shame of failing.

Restoring Relationship

Charlie needed to develop a relationship with the firefighter who prompted him to drink too much. After Charlie told me about how the drinking helped him forget the stresses of his job, I asked if he was open to getting to know the protector who prompted the drinking. He noticed that the first thing he heard was, "You are such an idiot for drinking too much again. Don't you ever think of how it impacts your wife and children?" Sounds like a familiar voice, doesn't it? The critical manager was back, and this time he was focused on the firefighter rather than the marketing consultant.

Charlie asked if the manager would be willing to give him space – to wait in the wings in our stage analogy – so he could connect with the firefighter. The manager was not ready to do that. He had more to say about the impact of the firefighter's behavior. Charlie needed to listen to him, to make sure that he felt heard, before he could turn his attention to the firefighter. As we get to know the members of our internal family, we will learn that the level of reactivity between them varies. When a firefighter's strategy causes some damage, there is often another part with a strong reaction. In order to build relationships with either of them, *both* of them need to feel heard and valued. The premise that each of them has a *positive intention*, no matter what behavior they provoke, helps to maintain an open heart toward each of them.

When Charlie turned toward the firefighter with curiosity and compassion for how much criticism he took for trying to suppress the pain, he began to build a relationship with him. He asked the firefighter to tell him more about what he feared would happen if he did not prompt Charlie to drink. Charlie learned that the firefighter shared the same fears as the manager; he did not want Charlie to be overwhelmed by shame and the belief that he was a failure. He also knew about the little boy who froze during the spelling bee.

By turning his attention inside after noticing the initial reaction to the idea of a marketing plan, Charlie gained valuable insight into the roles different members of his inner family played, as well as the relationship of the family members to one another. Very importantly, he got a glimpse of the vulnerable little boy holding the pain of shame and beliefs about being a failure. Ultimately, Charlie's work will include connecting directly with the little boy to help him release the burdens he has carried since that early experience. That requires the cooperation of his protectors, so the first step in the healing journey is to identify and build relationships with the protectors.

There are several key elements guiding the development of our relationships with our protectors, or what we can think of as *"befriending"* them.

The first step is to develop the habit of making a *"you-turn."*[114] This is the practice of turning our attention inside when we notice reactivity to something or someone. For Charlie, this happened when he reacted to the marketing plan and he noticed the critical voice and the shift in his posture. Turning our attention inside helps us to identify the presence of different parts of us, our family members, and their associated beliefs, emotions, images, and sensations.

After turning our attention inside and recognizing that a part or parts have surfaced, our next step is to *unblend* from it. We want to differentiate ourselves as leader of the family from the various members of the family. To assess whether we are unblended, we ask, "How am I feeling toward this member of my inner family? What kind of energy is flowing from me to this part? Is it loving, or is there some fear or frustration or confusion? Am I interested in connecting with it? How open is my heart to it? Do I have any curiosity about it? Do I notice any compassion for it? If we feel critical, fearful, or disinterested we are not ready to connect directly with the part. We first need to turn our attention to other parts that are present; it is their presence that blocks our innate ability as leader of the inner family to be loving.

The innate ability to be loving deserves emphasis. God is love (1 John 4:16), and we are made in his image (Genesis 1:26-27). When our intention is to connect with a member of our inner family, to establish a relationship, if we are not feeling loving – graciously accepting whatever is there just as it is – we know another part is present that holds its own feelings. Those feelings can be strong or subtle, so we need to take the time to notice our genuine response. We might hear criticism, or feel fear, or sense a desire to keep our distance, or get distracted. Myriad reactions occur, so it is also helpful to check for the presence of our innate resources – such as compassion, curiosity, clarity, or calm. Are we noticing the fruit of the Spirit? When those qualities guide our response to one of our inner family members, we know that we can begin to build a relationship.

In order to establish trust and safety, the bedrock of any good relationship, we want to be able to approach our inner family with as much unconditional acceptance as possible. If we have an agenda about how they should change, or stop doing what they are doing, or if we think they just need some advice, we are being led by other parts. Remember, this is the beginning of a relationship. Over time, there is an appropriate place for discussion about reactions that lead to problems, such as Charlie's drinking, but in the early stage of a relationship we need to ask parts that are frustrated, impatient, and fearful to stay over in the wings of the stage. This allows the one under the spotlight an opportunity to be heard and understood. A great question to ask ourselves is, *"Can I accept this member of my inner family just how it is right now, without needing it to change in some way?"*

The primary resource we bring to this phase of our healing journey is genuine *curiosity*. This is the curiosity that enables us to be open to whatever we learn when we turn our attention to a member of our inner family. Curiosity might not be the first thing we feel toward a part of our system. One of the many things people often notice when they turn their attention to their inner experience is that parts we can think of as "analysts" or "storytellers" (parts that know the details of our lives) tend to jump in and give us reasons for our reactions to things. But if we want to establish a relationship with the part that is actually *having* the reaction, we need to hear from it, not our analysts or storytellers. Imagine how you would feel if you were at a party getting to know someone and they asked you a question about yourself. Before you could respond someone else jumps in to answer for you. Would that make you want to share your own answer, or would you shrug and say, "Why bother?" We can affirm the valuable history known by storytellers, and the hypotheses offered by analysts, before we ask them to be observers.

With genuine curiosity we can begin to get to know more about a member of our inner family – why it shows up and how

Restoring Relationship

it hopes to help us. We can learn the positive intention it has for us, and eventually we will learn what it fears will happen if it stops doing what it has been doing. It is essential to realize that our protectors are *driven by fear*. In Charlie's case, his protectors feared the shame and pain from believing he was a failure would overwhelm him if they didn't either criticize him or numb him. Seeing how dedicated our protectors are to helping us opens us up even more for a loving relationship with them. As they feel appreciated, they tend to become more flexible and may be less intense in their reactions to threats. Just as we are getting to know them, they are getting to know the leader of the family. They are beginning to feel connected to the resources we possess as image-bearers. They begin to relax a bit as they recognize they are not alone. They also become more connected to the Holy Spirit, whose presence facilitates the leadership our inner family members need.

As I learned about this way of understanding ourselves I often thought of Jesus interacting with the wide array of people he encountered during his public ministry. He turned *toward* people, including people who did not have the courage to speak their needs aloud, offering relationship. My favorite example is the woman "who had been subject to bleeding for twelve years" (Luke 8:40-56). Her story exemplifies some of the key qualities involved in healing: connection, courage, compassion, patience, and persistence.

A synagogue leader "fell at Jesus' feet, pleading with him to come to his house because his only daughter, a girl of about twelve, was dying." The man was clearly desperate for help; his only daughter, a girl on the cusp of womanhood with so much of her future before her, lay on her deathbed. Jesus set out for the man's house, making his way through a crowd that "almost crushed him." A woman in the crowd who was afflicted by unrelenting bleeding, a condition that rendered her unclean and outcast from society, touched Jesus' cloak, and he "felt the power" go out of him. It took persistence to make her way to him through the throng of people and courage to touch his cloak, a violation of the strict rules forbidding contact with the "unclean." Jesus immediately stopped to learn more despite the urgency of his mission. Jesus often surprises me with his patience. Something important happened, and, rather than rushing to the next demand, he paused to connect with the woman. Singled out from the crowd, she fearfully told the story of her affliction and healing. She was the recipient of the power Jesus referred to – the power of compassion for her suffering.

I have a sense that this crowd was filled with people desperate for Jesus' help. Peter was confused by Jesus' question about someone touching him; he reminded him, "the people are crowding and pressing against you." I wonder how they felt about a woman who was not supposed to get close to people, who should not have been in that crowd at all, being bold enough to touch this revered teacher and healer? Some no doubt thought, "How dare she?" One of the synagogue leaders had made a request of Jesus; certainly his needs were the priority. Yet, Jesus stopped and turned his full attention to the woman, praising her for the faith that led to her healing – faith that relationship with Jesus was what she needed.

"While Jesus was still speaking" a man from the synagogue leader's house ran up to report that his daughter had died, so he should not "bother the teacher anymore." Not only did the woman violate customs by being in the crowd, she might be responsible for the girl's death! I imagine many in the crowd felt anger and fear and even hopelessness. Jesus calmly reassured them, "Don't be afraid; just believe, and she will be healed." Jesus "took her by the hand" and the girl's "spirit returned." In this story we hear echoes of Psalm 31: "Into your hands I commit my spirit; redeem me, O Lord, the God of truth" (Psalm 31:5). Jesus holds us, and we can join him in holding the tender parts of our soul to bring healing and redemption.

Where we fear scarcity, Jesus shows abundance: abundant time, compassion, and patience for our seemingly unrelenting needs. As image-bearers, we possess these same qualities. We can also open space to bring in more of the power of the Holy Spirit as we connect with parts that would otherwise crowd our inner space. We have the capacity to lead our inner family, joining with Jesus in turning toward the hurting, desperate, hopeless, and fearful parts of ourselves to connect with them, to bring Jesus' presence to them for healing. As a first step, the following exercise will help you get to know one of your own protectors.

****

Exercise
Befriending a Protector

Think of a recent time when you reacted to a situation in a manner that left you unsettled. I encourage you to choose a situation where your reaction was in the range of a "3" on a 0 to 10 scale where 10 is the most reactive you can imagine being. Perhaps you found yourself replaying the incident over and over again. You could have been left with tension in your body after the interaction, or a sense of frustration, embarrassment, or even shame over the way you responded to someone.

When you have the incident in mind, shift your attention inside of yourself and notice what is present. Thoughts, emotions, images, and sensations are all elements of memory and any one of these, or a combination of several elements, can surface when we recall something distressing.

Bring your attention to whatever is most intense or vivid. Notice how you feel toward the part of you that holds the thoughts, emotions, images, or sensations related to the incident you are recalling. This member of your inner family is giving you information; notice whether you are open to learning more. It helps to remember that all parts have a *positive intention*, no matter how they appear.

Often, another part will block your curiosity. Our inner family members rarely show up alone; recall Paul's lament about his conflicting impulses. If you are not feeling curious about learning more, simply ask whether whoever is blocking your curiosity would be willing to give you some space. You might want to breathe in at the same time, bringing spaciousness and creating room for more of the Spirit. When we intentionally breathe in slowly and deeply we can think of welcoming more of the Spirit, enhancing our ability to attend to our inner experience with grace and loving-kindness. We never want to force our way into our inner relationships. As you breathe in spaciousness, creating room for all of the family members who need your attention, notice whether there is any sense of pressure, or a sense of pushing a particular part to step back. If so, that is a part that might need your attention first. Our spiritual practice is to cultivate patient persistence with a goal of bringing loving attention to whomever is in need.

After asking the part that is blocking your connection to give you space, notice whether you feel some spaciousness, and ask yourself again if you are open and curious. If so, bring your attention to whatever you notice – thoughts, emotions, images, and/or sensations. Pause for a moment just to be with what you are noticing. You can welcome it and let it know you are curious about it. Then pause again to see what arises.

In developing relationships with our inner family members, open-ended questions help us express our curiosity toward them. You can try asking things such as, "How are you trying to help me?" "What do you hope will happen?" "What are you afraid will happen if you don't do what you are doing?" "What do you need from me?"

Sometimes a part will not respond to questions. Notice if you are still open and curious, and if so, try just being with the part and extending grace to it without any expectation or agenda. Often, this kind of connection is very calming to a part. You might notice that sensations ease and you feel more spacious inside.

Practicing the "you-turn," turning your attention inside with curiosity when you have a reaction to a person or situation, is an ideal way to befriend your team of protectors. When you are exploring your inner system on your own, you might encounter a fierce protector who is not open to relationship with you and is

Part III – A New Spiritual Practice

unwilling to allow space for connection to any other inner family members. It helps to remember that the degree of energy our protectors use to keep pain away is roughly equal to the intensity of the pain. A fierce protector is very afraid of the pain, and realizing how dedicated that protector is can cultivate our compassion. Bringing loving presence to it, as many times as necessary, is a wonderful spiritual practice.*

---

* Please see Appendix A on page 207 for a detailed description of the spiritual practice.

Chapter Twelve
BEFRIENDING OUR EXILES

Paula looked discouraged when she walked into my office. She told me about yet another difficult conversation with her mother. When Paula reported on interactions with her mother she often noticed a protector who wanted to cut off and not have any relationship with her mother at all. In previous sessions she befriended this protector; it began to trust her leadership and became more flexible about allowing her to connect with her mother. After the most recent phone call, rather than wanting just to give up on the relationship, Paula said she felt depressed. She had difficulty getting out of bed in the morning and had little energy to tend to her responsibilities. The tears flowed as she shared this with me.

Paula was open to being present to the sadness; the protectors in her system were relaxed enough to allow her to be with whomever was carrying the grief over her relationship with her mother. As she focused on the sadness and a heavy sensation in her chest she got an image of a young girl being told, "I never wanted you. I was already overwhelmed with three children and did not want to get pregnant again." She recalled times when she was told that she was "not brilliant" like her siblings. Despite having two master's degrees and speaking multiple languages, Paula had a part of herself that firmly believed her intellect fell short of the family standard. She felt compassion for the little girl who carried the sadness, and, as she connected with her more deeply, she learned that the girl believed she was "unwanted," "unworthy," and "not good enough." Few things provoke as much pain as beliefs such as these. They reflect a sense of *defectiveness* – that something is broken beyond repair.

This little girl is an example of an *exile*, a member of the inner family who carries burdens from adverse experiences. Burdens include negative beliefs, painful emotions, distressing images, and intense sensations. Burdens threaten the wellbeing of the whole system, so our managerial protectors work proactively to keep them from surfacing, and our firefighter protectors react when they do surface. The goal of our protectors is to keep these parts *exiled*, locked up in the basement of our family home.[115] Protectors are driven by fear – fear of what will happen if the most vulnerable members of our inner family escape from exile. They often fear we will be overwhelmed by the pain held by exiles or that a deep dark secret will be exposed. That is why we first connect with our protectors to establish a trusting relationship before we attempt to connect with our exiles. Our protectors need to know the leader of the system, to feel our calm and confident presence as we offer hope for healing the pain held by exiles. Calm and confidence are two of the many resources we bring as the leader of our inner family when we are in harmony with the Holy Spirit.

The little girl in Paula's system had been isolated with her pain for many, many years. The young exiles in our inner family are like the children in Jesus' day. They were the most vulnerable in society, subject to high mortality rates, and even infanticide and abandonment.[116] Jesus corrected the disciples who, like their society, thought children were not worth his time and attention. "Let the little children come to me and do not hinder them, for the kingdom of God belongs to such as these" (Luke 18:16). Jesus inverted the presumed order of importance of adults over children, and he tied receiving the kingdom of God to receiving little children (Luke 18:17). In the context of these verses, "receiving children" means extending hospitality to them, performing the same actions – washing feet, anointing their heads with oil, a kiss of greeting – as would be offered to adults.[117] The exiled members of our inner family are as worthy of time and attention as any other person, but that has not been their experience.

Throughout Jesus' ministry, he surprised people by treating the marginalized members of society with compassion and respect, recognizing them as equally worthy of healing and redemption. The tendency to categorize and prioritize some people and groups over others reflects the work of protectors, whether it happens in our inner family or in our external relationships and culture. It can be challenging to maintain the perspective that protectors are well-intentioned when we notice our own prejudice or bias. When confronted with attitudes that are not consistent with Jesus' example, we have an opportunity to do a "you-turn." We turn our attention inside and connect with the protector who has a bias or prejudice. Inevitably, we will learn about an exile they are protecting; when the exile is healed protectors can release the beliefs that erect barriers between ourselves and others. Each time this happens a constraint to our innate loving connection is released, freeing us to relate to others as Jesus did.

Little ones who have been exiled for years have been cut off from the loving relationship they desperately need. When Paula expressed compassion for the little girl's pain and let her know she could tell Paula all about how it had been for her, the little girl was initially reticent. Paula had an image of the girl with her back turned. I encouraged Paula to just be with the little girl and extend compassion from her heart. The value of patiently extending compassion cannot be overstated. Picture a scene where this little girl sees Paula for the first time: she notices the love in Paula's eyes and feels the warmth of her grace. The light of Paula's love begins to dissipate the fog of shame. So much healing happens in that time of connection.

It is not unusual for protectors to step back in when we make contact with exiles. They hold so much fear about what will happen when the pain of the exiles is uncovered that, even if they were initially willing to allow a relationship with the exile, they often change their minds and return to block it. Sometimes it is very obvious a protector has returned; you might hear, "That's the dumbest thing ever. Why is she so sensitive about that!?" Other times it is far subtler. We might notice a sense that it was not that big a deal; after all, we tell ourselves, many children have far worse circumstances. This is an example of a protector who minimizes, a very common member of the inner family. It is difficult to accept that when we are young we make meaning of situations that might seem exaggerated or irrational as we mature. Parts of us can spend a lot of time comparing ourselves with others who "had it worse." When we are getting to know our exiles it is imperative that we identify and connect with protectors who want to minimize, compare, and dismiss the exile's experience. The goal is not to ascertain with 100% certainty what happened to the exile; that is impossible without a video recording. The goal is to connect and accept the *meaning* the exile made of the circumstances.

Paula checked to see if any protectors were blocking her compassion and curiosity and did not feel that was the case. Yet, the little girl still seemed reluctant to connect with her. This is also common. The little girl had been alone with her pain for many years, and despite the loving-kindness Paula extended to her, she did not trust it. Why should she? She had never had an experience like that before. The adults in her life were not trustworthy; they did not meet her needs. This is where patience is very important. Approaching exiles can be like approaching an animal in the wild; we enter their space carefully and calmly, with the understanding that they might never have encountered someone who is safe. It can take many visits with them to establish trust.

When a safe, trusting connection is established, we invite the exile to share whatever they want us to know about what life was like for them. The exile is often a very young part of our system, but can be any age. Throughout the process we are noticing if we can remain totally open to whatever they need to share without any sense of dismissing the importance of it or denying the reality of their experience.

Because exiled parts often share painful experiences and emotions related to their primary caregivers, protective parts might feel guilty about what they define as "blaming the parent." It is important to turn to this protector and reassure it that the exile is just sharing the meaning it made of the experience. The assumption is that the vast majority of parents are doing the best they can, but unfortunately, that does not prevent children from making meaning of their circumstances that becomes a burden of painful beliefs and emotions. When we can connect without any judgment or fear, for the first time an exile experiences what they needed originally. They feel loving acceptance, compassion for their distress, and hope that the burden they have carried for so long can be lifted. They experience what Jesus offers all of us.

If we are exploring our inner family on our own, initial connection with our exiles is likely as far as we can successfully go. Even that can be difficult because of the numerous protectors who surface because of fears of what the exiles hold. Each person's system is different, and there will be different stages of the journey where working with someone trained in the Internal Family Systems (IFS) model can facilitate healing.* Generally, the more adverse experiences that occurred in childhood, and the more trauma experienced over the years, the more difficult it will be to connect with the exiles in our inner family on our own. I cannot overstate the value of patience in this process. There is tremendous benefit in connecting with our protectors, even if that is all we can do without professional help. We will often notice more calm and flexibility as we build relationships with protectors. Transformation is not a task to be checked off of a list, but a lifelong process that does not unfold without setbacks

---

* To find an IFS therapist or practitioner in your area see *www.IFS-Institute.com*. IFS training is available to therapists and other helping professionals.

and challenges. When we understand that transformation is not about having an agenda for change that *must* occur, rather an intention for healing that occurs with time spent in relationship, we can embrace this practice of connecting with our inner family as a spiritual discipline.

We can accept the offer Jesus extended. "Come to me, all you who are weary and burdened, and I will give you rest. Take my yoke upon you and learn from me, for I am gentle and humble in heart, and you will find rest for your souls" (Matthew 11:28-29). Yoked together with Jesus, and yoked together with our hard-working protectors and our vulnerable exiles, we can find rest for our souls. We can learn to trust the loving presence that patiently builds a relationship, accepting us right where we are and helping us heal along the way.

The initial connection with our exiles begins their healing process. When working with a therapist trained in the IFS model, there are additional healing steps that the therapist facilitates with exiles. The therapist is trained to be a "parts detector" to assist with identifying protectors who can disrupt the relationship between clients and their exiles. It is critical for an exile to be able to share everything they need us to know about their experience, so the therapist ensures there is no pressure or rushing while a person is witnessing the world of the exile. There is an *intention* for healing, but not an *agenda* about it happening in a certain way or timeframe. When the exile feels fully understood, an offer is extended to them to leave the time and place where they have been stuck since the distressing events took place. It is very freeing for the exile to have the freedom to leave a time and place where they experienced adversity, to be in a space they choose that is safe and comfortable. Now that you have a relationship with them, they often want to be with you in the present. It is their choice and theirs alone; they are no longer subject to others' control and are no longer relegated to the metaphorical basement of the family home.

After leaving the time and place where painful experiences occurred, a ritual is performed to allow the exile to release the burdens they have held for so long. Throughout Scripture rituals mark important events in the relationship of God and his people.[118] A ritual helps to honor and release each component of the burden left from adversity. It has been very interesting to see the creative ways exiles choose to release burdens. One option is to use the elements – earth, air, fire, or water – as receptacles for the beliefs, emotions, images, and sensations carried by our exiles. I think of these as the core elements of God's creation, each of which contains special power for transformation. Some clients choose to give their burden to Jesus or to send it into the light of his presence. The ritual is a turning point for exiles. When they bury burdens deep in the earth, send them into the air to be carried away on the wind, allow fire to consume them, dissolve them in water, or offer them to the light that transforms darkness there is a deep sense of relief. The burdens are heavy, and releasing them brings freedom.

After a member of our internal family releases the burdens they have held, they are now ready to reclaim the qualities they were originally meant to contribute to the inner family. The burdens blocked those qualities, so we simply invite them to notice what they would like to reclaim. Because many exiles are young, their healing often restores qualities we associate with young children such as creativity, playfulness, spontaneity, freedom, the joy of learning and creating, and unrestrained exuberance. We celebrate the restoration of their given nature – their return from exile. This is the moment of redemption, where the exile experiences the promise that ultimately nothing can separate us from God's love.

These beautiful verses in Isaiah show God's care for the exiles:

> Do not fear, for I have redeemed you; I have summoned you by name; you are mine. When you pass through the waters, I will be with you; and when you pass through the rivers, they will not sweep over you. When you walk through the fire, you will not be burned; the flames will not set you ablaze. For I am the Lord your God, the Holy One of Israel, your Savior...Do not be afraid, for I am with you..." (Isaiah 43:1-3, 5).

Imagine God saying this to one of your exiles. Better yet, say them out loud with one of your tender young parts in mind. In these verses God is promising the Israelites that he will deliver them. There is no condition, just grace. The most striking characteristic of God is "free, self-giving love."[119] The deliverance from exile reflects his unceasing concern for our well-being.[120] When we join God in seeking out our tender, burdened exiles, we join this mission of redemption, of freedom. We share in the ministry of grace so all members of our inner family experience the loving embrace of knowing, "you are mine."

The exile's journey of healing does not happen in isolation. The protectors who worked to keep a particular exile's experience

Restoring Relationship

from overwhelming the system watch carefully as the exile tells their story and releases their burdens. After an exile heals, protectors are given the opportunity to consider whether they still need to do the job they have been doing. Sometimes a protector is eager to give up a job and do something more fun. Other times they relax and express more flexibility, but are not quite ready to give up a job entirely. One of the most important steps in the healing process is to remain in relationship with both the exile and their protectors. Any new relationship requires time and attention to strengthen. Because our neural networks hold memories, in this process we intentionally connect with the networks holding adverse experiences and form a new network holding the experience of loving connection. Reinforcing that tender new network is critical to create lasting change. Spending time daily with our inner family members is a key practice supporting the transformation of our inner world.

****

Exercise
Befriending an Exile

I offer this exercise for a time when you are ready to connect with one of your exiles. The time might not be now. It is very important to be patient, connecting with protectors as long as it takes until they trust you to turn toward an exile. This also might not be something you can do on your own. When there is greater adversity in life there will be more protectors and they will be more determined to keep the pain of exiles from surfacing.

When you sense that you have an open heart toward a member of your inner family who experienced adversity, set an intention to establish a relationship with this exile. Notice what arises: thoughts, emotions, images, sensations – or any combination of those elements. Repeatedly ask yourself whether you remain open to this vulnerable one. Practice patience when a protector resurfaces. Sometimes they just seem to need to let us know they are watching, but will quickly step back. Other times they need more time and attention before allowing connection with an exile. It helps to remind ourselves that *all* connection is healing. Any part of our system that we greet with loving presence will experience some degree of healing.

When you are able to be with an exile, the goal is simply to extend grace, curiosity, compassion, and love. Sometimes it takes repeated visits to establish trust. The younger the exile was when they experienced adversity, the more likely they are to have difficulty trusting. Consistently spending time with them builds trust so that, at the right time, they can allow you to witness all they experienced, release their burdens, and reclaim their unique gifts.

As you practice building relationships with your inner family members by greeting them with acceptance and curiosity, you will notice that protectors are increasingly willing to allow you to connect with exiles.

Patience is indispensable to this process, but patience is one of the resources we possess that gets blocked by our protectors. Protective members of the inner family often get impatient with symptoms and issues and try to force healing to happen. They might be very insistent about connecting with an exile. But if these impatient parts (who have an agenda about how fast healing needs to occur) jump in and take the lead, the protectors who are committed to doing the job of keeping our painful burdens locked down will harden their stance. When you notice this happening (when you feel a shift away from calm, confident, curious openness), turn toward the one with the agenda. Offer them your presence and learn what they fear will happen if healing takes time.

We want to approach building relationships with inner family members with the attitude that each one of them is worthy of time and attention. The goal is to hold an intention for healing without pursuing an agenda about how and when that needs to happen. Intention feels spacious, calm, and curious. There is an expectant, but patient, openness to whatever unfolds. When we have an agenda, there is a sense of striving, and we will probably notice energy in our body pushing us toward a goal.

Building relationships with our inner family is a spiritual *practice*. Commitment to this practice supports the process of transformation. Transformation occurs as we lead our inner family in harmony with the Spirit, patiently and persistently connecting with all who need our loving attention.

Chapter Thirteen
GUIDING PRINCIPLES FOR BUILDING RELATIONSHIPS

While we explored the idea of building relationships with our inner family members, a core principle guided the process. Namely, as image-bearers we possess intrinsic resources for healing no matter what happened in our life and what legacy we were born into. The things we experience, both as a result of others' choices and our own, cannot erase our inherent qualities. Rather, we have seen that life experiences cause protective parts to take on roles that block those qualities, and exiled parts carry burdens that *inhibit* their gifts from being available. Healing is a process of building trusting relationships to *release the constraints* to our resources so that all members of the inner family are free to contribute their essential qualities.

A related principle is that there is no limit to these resources. We do not have to fear scarcity. There will be sufficient compassion or courage or patience for the journey of healing. The Spirit's presence brings unlimited "love, joy, peace, patience, kindness, goodness, faithfulness, gentleness and self-control" (Galatians 5:22). This is not an exhaustive list of the Spirit's qualities, but a representative sampling of the incredible wealth of resources available to us. In developing the IFS model, Richard Schwartz discovered that eight "C's" described the healing presence he witnessed in clients.[121] It is a helpful list, dovetailing with the fruit of the Spirit: curiosity, calm, compassion, creativity, courage, connection, clarity and confidence. He also noticed five "P's" including patience, persistence, presence, playfulness and perspective. When we remember that we were created for relationship, it makes sense to accept that we have these intrinsic, inexhaustible resources, all of which make loving relationships possible.

These are the resources we bring to bear when we lead our internal family in harmony with the Holy Spirit. Our spiritual practice shifts from *working hard to develop something we think we lack* to building relationships with the members of the inner family that *block the expression of something we already have*.

Another guiding principle is that restoring connection and building relationships that heal begins within ourselves. Typically, the emphasis in our spiritual communities has been either on relationship with God or with others. It is a new practice to make a "you-turn" each time we notice something inconsistent with our values, when we notice sin of some kind. Most of us have a protector in our system who is very good at pointing out others' flaws and coming up with detailed plans for all of the ways others could change in order to make our life easier. When we expend our energy in making those plans or in telling others about them, we are left frustrated or disappointed because they do not create change. It can be incredibly encouraging to turn inward to learn about the protective strategies that impact our relationships with others, and the underlying vulnerability that gives rise to those strategies. As we do so, we feel a shift. Resources like calm, clarity, and compassion start bubbling up, and we begin seeing others in a new light. We begin to understand that they have protectors and exiles too. The parts of them with which we have difficulty are not the full representation of who they are.

When I first met with Brenda, she was completely overwhelmed by her responsibilities for her disabled son. There had been challenges throughout his life, but the transition to adolescence presented new issues. Her husband's distance had always been a source of disappointment, but as her son matured physically, she began to hear her husband making assumptions about their son's ability to live independently that she thought were completely unrealistic. She was bewildered and anxious when her husband talked about their son going to college and living on his own; from her perspective, and that of the many professionals involved in his care, those were not realistic hopes for him.

As Brenda spent time noticing the different parts of her system who were provoked by her husband's comments and behavior, she met a protector who worked tirelessly to meet her husband's needs, a protector who believed that if she did everything perfectly he might notice her efforts and appreciate them. She learned that there was another protector who was not at all happy about that strategy. The second protector was angry and wanted Brenda to confront her husband about the ways he was falling short.

It is not unusual to find "polarities" in our inner family – parts who have opposing ideas about things. While these two protectors had different jobs, they were both very focused on her husband. When protectors focus on another person, they do so because the person provokes an exile. Remember, protectors fear

Restoring Relationship

the burdens our exiles hold so their strategies are always a reflection of those fears. In Brenda's case, her relationship with her husband provoked young parts of her who held painful emotions and beliefs from times when her father expected her to perform perfectly with little emotional support. Rather than focusing solely on her husband, we shifted to a process of working with her protectors to establish their trust, then developed a healing relationship with the young parts of her that carried burdens from their experiences.

The process of working with Brenda's protectors and exiles freed up the energy her protectors had consumed. When those protectors were in charge, they blocked her clarity, courage, and compassion. But she needed all three to make important decisions about her son's future, to take a stand that differed from her husband's desires, and to connect with her husband in his struggle over the loss of the future he hoped for his son. After making the "you-turn" and developing relationships with key members of her inner family, Brenda noticed the return of the clarity, courage, and compassion needed for navigating the difficult season with her husband and son.

While the work we do individually does not guarantee that important people in our lives will do anything different, in Brenda's case she noticed that the shift inside translated to a shift in the dynamic with her husband. Calm is one of the most helpful resources freed up by relating to our parts. Calm is contagious, just as anxiety is contagious. When we connect with family members from a calm place, difficult decisions and conversations can be much more productive. And even before Brenda was ready to discuss things with her husband, *she* experienced more calm and confidence and less anxiety, a change that was very encouraging for her.

Our paradigm shifts when we realize that we possess the resources we need for relationships, that there is no limit to them, and that the journey of healing begins within ourselves. While it is not uncommon to have a protector who is disappointed that the focus is not on someone else, validating the disappointment and turning inside to get to know our inner family ultimately brings freedom and healing. Parker Palmer says, "Self-care is never a selfish act – it is simply good stewardship of the only gift I have, the gift I was put on earth to offer others. Anytime we can listen to true self and give the care it requires, we do it not only for ourselves, but for the many others whose lives we touch."[122]

The most important guiding principle of all is "there is no fear in love. But perfect love drives out fear..."(1 John 4:18). Fear is driven out *not because it is judged or unwelcome, but because it is embraced, understood, and transformed*. I think of a drop of detergent falling on oily water. It is a gentle but powerful force. God's presence lives in us, both because we are image-bearers and because of the limitless power of the Holy Spirit. This presence is the calming grace that patiently welcomes our fearful parts and facilitates relationships that transform fear to confidence, clarity, joy, and freedom. "First we were loved, now we love" (1 John 4:19, The Message). We extend love each time we turn toward our protective parts, accepting their fears as valid because they come from our protectors' limited perspective. We extend love each time we welcome the hurting, vulnerable, timid ones in our inner family. And when we extend love, our fear and pain are transformed into love. The spiritual practice of building relationships with our inner family members is like weaving on a loom. Each time the shuttle passes from side to side the fabric grows stronger. Each time we connect with loving and welcoming presence, the bonds with our inner family members strengthen. Gradually we notice the dissipation of fear and the reemergence of the innate qualities reflecting God's character, preparing us to love others as we have experienced love.

In building relationships with our inner family members we are practicing the greatest commandment, to "love the Lord your God with all your heart and with all your soul and with all your mind and with all your strength" (Mark 12:28-31). Leading from our soul, where we possess the qualities that reflect God's character, we lovingly attend to our thoughts, our emotions, our memories, and the sensations in our body. We restore relationship and transform fear and pain. And with God's help, we embrace the freedom to love our neighbors as ourselves.

Part Four

LOVING OTHERS AS WE LOVE OURSELVES

Chapter Fourteen
SEASONS OF LOSS

Tears filled Mary's eyes as she began telling me about her best friend Shelly's death. They spilled over, running silently down her cheeks while she shared the story of the friendship, spanning more than 30 years. Mary spoke fondly of the time when she had two young children close in age and Shelly would come with her to run errands. Laughing, she said one of her girls looked so much like Shelly people assumed they were mother and daughter. She smiled as she told me about their mutual love of fun parties, vacationing together, and their ability to drop by at any time because they lived just two blocks apart. Through the tears Mary said, "I'm trying to be strong."

There it was again, a message that is ubiquitous in our culture – the message that the appropriate response to loss is to "be strong." I was watching a TV show while writing this chapter and a character said to herself, "You don't need broken right now; you need strength." The character was reacting to her child's disability and felt that she was letting her husband down because she was tearful. A few months ago I saw an interview with Cindy McCain, widow of John McCain, on the anniversary of his death.

She acknowledged the challenges of grieving but her final comment echoed Mary's – her emphasis was on being strong. When you listen for it, you will hear the message.

My experience, including the four years I worked at a hospice, taught me that "strong" in our culture is defined as stoic. Strong means not being "overly emotional," moving on with life, getting over the loss quickly, and shielding others from the pain resulting from the loss. Mary told me that only six weeks after her friend's death a mutual friend told her to "get it together" because she was "still crying" when speaking of their friend. I recall a client at the hospice sharing that three weeks after her husband of over 50 years died a neighbor asked her when she was going to start dating! It is not easy to believe that feeling our emotions is acceptable when messages like these are the norm, not the exception. Some messages are indirect. When a friend does not ask about a loss, or colleagues expect a return to work and full productivity regardless of a loss, or a loss is dismissed with an offhand comment, the grieving person hears, "Get over it."

Why is being "strong" or "getting over it" the goal?

The goal of protectors is to block what they fear. Loss results in painful emotions that provoke fear: fear of being overwhelmed, fear of not "getting over it," fear of being alone with this burden. Fear is the motivating force for our protectors, who are hard at work during seasons of loss. Grief is one of the painful emotions our protectors learn to stifle. Other people's protectors echo their message about the importance of moving on, limiting the season of grief, and keeping our emotions under wraps. The message to "be strong" reverberates; we hear it within ourselves and we hear it from many people outside of us. It is not easy to hear the "gentle whisper" (1 Kings 19:11-13) of God's voice, of our own compassion and courage, in the midst of the strident message from protectors.

The strength of the protective messages about grief reveals the magnitude of the fear we have about it. The most common fear of protectors is that we will be overwhelmed by the burdens held by our exiles.[123] It seems that in our culture, protectors see loss as putting us at very high risk for being overwhelmed. One of the reasons loss runs the risk of being overwhelming is that we do not allow ourselves to experience grief over the course of our lives as we suffer loss. Any time we experience loss and cut off from our grief (when protectors are successful in exiling it) the burden of loss held in our system grows. It does not dissipate with time unless we use the time to intentionally work through our grief, as I learned when I worked with Betty.

I met Betty when I worked at a hospice. She was having a great deal of difficulty functioning following the death of her husband. They had been married over 50 years, so it was understandable that she would be experiencing loneliness and sadness. However, Betty's symptoms were both more intense and more pervasive than would be expected. She experienced severe anxiety and had little energy for even basic activities such as hygiene and eating. She wept most of the time and was anguished over the impact of her grief on her daughters, feeling shame over being dependent on them for emotional support. As her story unfolded I learned that her father abruptly left the family when Betty was 13. She grew up in the Northeast and spoke of the very strong message she received about not showing any emotion. She was mystified about her father's departure; there was no discussion about reasons and no further contact with him. Later in life, Betty's first marriage ended in divorce. She had two young children and had to return to the workforce to support them. Once again, there was no space for grief.

I can appreciate how hard her protectors must have been working through those heartbreaking seasons. As a child, her protectors got the message that a good girl would not burden her mother by showing emotion, and as an adult they had to keep her going in order to care for her children. Unfortunately, the well-intentioned protectors made sure that all of Betty's considerable grief was buried, and each time she experienced loss there was a new layer of sediment piling up inside. When her husband died the container simply could not hold any more grief; her protectors' worst fear was realized. She was overwhelmed by grief. None of the grief provoked by her considerable losses was ever allowed to surface and it became a subterranean pool of hot magma just waiting to erupt. Grief simply does not dissipate unless it is met with compassion, given space and time, and is allowed to be expressed. Grief from 70 years earlier was as fresh for Betty as grief from her recent loss, showing both how successful protectors can be in exiling grief, and also how true it is that time alone will not heal it.

It is essential for all of us to learn to work with the protectors we encounter during seasons of loss because, unlike some of the other common causes of distress we will explore, loss is a universal experience. Loss is at the heart of the story in Genesis 3. As a result of the attempt to gain autonomy, to be less dependent on God, the intimacy humans enjoyed with God in the Garden of Eden is lost.[124] In choosing autonomy, death became an imminent threat.[125] A threat to our survival is the most frightening threat we encounter. "We are all born outside Eden";[126] we are all born with the burden of the loss of perfect intimacy with God and the threat of death. What could be a greater loss and a greater threat to our wellbeing? We come into this life holding the pain of the loss of intimacy with God as well as the intense fear of death. We all share this exile, this most vulnerable grieving and terrified member of our internal family.

At whatever point our system becomes aware of this exile, inner family members will valiantly take on the job of protecting the system from what it holds. Perhaps these protectors are on the job even from the womb. We are primed to avoid grief and the terror of our greatest existential threat. Just as this first experience of loss is universal, subsequent losses are also inevitable. Loss comes in many forms. We sometimes think only of death, but as we saw in Betty's case, abandonment and divorce are also forms of loss. Such things as infertility, financial issues, and barriers to education and career advancement represent the loss of hopes and dreams. Military deployment and frequent moves can disrupt family life and result in loss. It is rare to avoid the loss of belonging; friend groups typically shift and, like a game of musical chairs, someone is left standing. As with any emotional experience, loss is subjective not objective. Myriad experiences can result in a sense of loss; what provokes grief for me might not for you, and vice versa. Multiple losses can occur either simultaneously or sequentially, compounding the impact. For example, divorce can result in financial loss and the loss of community if a family is forced to move as a result of the change in financial condition.

The emotional impact of loss is not limited to sadness. When loss is accompanied by a sense of abandonment, fear can rise to the level of terror. Sometimes there is a sense of despair and hopelessness. Certain types of loss can also result in a sense of relief, such as the death of a loved one following prolonged illness. On the heels of relief many experience guilt, worrying that they are betraying their loved one in feeling relieved. For some, anger will emerge as one of the layers of their grief process. Anger can be held by protectors who are avoiding the vulnerability of sadness, or it can be a response to a loss experienced through injustice such as racism.

Emotions are often accompanied by negative beliefs such as, "It's my fault," "I'm unlovable," "I'm alone," "I'm broken." These beliefs tend to be statements about our worth, statements that leave no room for any other truth about ourselves. They provoke shame and pain, causing protectors to double down on their efforts to keep us from connecting with the vulnerable parts holding these beliefs.

The dizzying array of emotions and beliefs that arise in response to loss do not come and go in a predictable pattern. There are many different models to help us understand the process of bereavement, but they tend to focus on the loss of a loved one. While it is tempting to apply one of those models to our experience, I encourage you to see whether viewing the experience through the lens of the IFS model might be most helpful. With the perspective that we have vulnerable exiles holding experiences of loss, and their associated hard-working protectors helping us to continue to function through the journey of grieving a loss, we can turn our attention to what we, or someone we hope to support, is *actually* experiencing at a given time without any preconceived notions of what "should" be happening.

When we can bring curiosity in focusing on our own inner family, or that of a friend who is in a season of loss, we can establish a relationship with the protectors who are working so hard to mitigate the impact of grief. Our curiosity sends the message that they are welcome, no matter what their strategy is to protect us. Some of the common protectors we might encounter include:

- *"Critics"* who step in when emotions surface to echo the cultural message that there is something wrong with us for feeling those emotions;
- *"Distancers"* who prompt us to withdraw and isolate, fearing the reaction others have to grief;
- *"Needy"* parts who cling to others, fearing being alone with their grief;
- Various *"firefighters"* who use strategies to numb the pain such as overuse of alcohol, food and other distractions;
- *"Distractors"* who use various strategies to shift our focus away from grief; and
- *"Spiritual"* parts who dismiss grief by asserting the loss was "God's will" or "God's plan."

I want to reiterate that the "names" of the above protectors reveal their *strategies*, not their *essence*. When hurting exiles are healed, protective parts are freed up to bring their own intrinsic qualities to the system. For example, a "distancer" could morph into a part who has clarity about appropriate boundaries in relationships. It is never the intention to "get rid of" parts; the intention is to facilitate healing so we have access to all of the resources they possess.

Restoring Relationship

The ubiquitous message to limit the expression of grief – both the intensity of emotions and the length of time spent grieving – makes sense when we realize we all share the legacy of the original loss of intimacy with God and when we consider the numerous ways we experience loss throughout life. We have protectors we must befriend in order to be able to respond to loss in a way that is healing. They are doing their best to help us, and they deserve our compassion and respect. Turning our attention to our inner family members and welcoming whatever they hold – beliefs, emotions, images, and sensations – is an act of grace. It is countercultural because we are letting them know, as leader of the inner family, we can handle what they are experiencing, which has a powerfully calming effect. I have repeatedly worked with very dedicated and intense protectors who do not believe what seems paradoxical to them – that when we connect with a part holding something intense the part will actually calm down, not overwhelm the system. With patient and persistent contact, validating their concerns and reassuring them that connection will bring calm, they will gradually allow the space to facilitate relationship. Whether the loss is our own or that of someone coming to us for support, our first step is to make a "you-turn," shifting our focus inside, opening our curiosity about how loss has impacted our internal family.

Exercise
Befriending Protectors Related to Loss

When you have quiet time in a private space let your inner family know that your intention is to explore your experience with loss. You might want to have a sheet of paper and something to write with; depicting the different family members that emerge around a particular issue helps to build relationships with them. You can use different colors and shapes to represent them, you can write down the thoughts and beliefs of different parts, and you can notice the sequence in which parts emerge.

When we set an intention, such as exploring an experience with loss, protective parts will often react. Notice what happens for you when you let your inner family know that you are curious about a time when you experienced loss. Possible responses include:
- Body sensations such as tightness in the chest or abdomen, constriction in the throat, or tears in your eyes.
- Emotions such as fear, anger, sadness, regret, or confusion.
- Thoughts such as, "Why stir up something painful?" "I'm over this so what's the point?" "It's weak to wallow in grief. Don't go there."

Bring your attention to whatever seems most present, and ask yourself if your heart is open to it. In other words, can you accept it *without needing it to be different in any way*? If not, there is a second part blocking your ability to connect with the first one you turned toward. Notice the reaction that part is having to your interest in the other part. There could be fear. You might go blank as soon as you try to focus, or you might hear something like, "Don't go there. There's no point." Whatever is blocking your connection, let it know that you feel its concern. Tell it that you just want to connect with the other part to understand how it is trying to help you, and ask if it would be willing to make space so you can do that. Often you will feel a softening; when you turn back to the first part and ask yourself, "How am I feeling toward it now?" you will notice you are curious or compassionate.

When you are able to connect with the original part from a place of curiosity, spend time with it. Remember, you are developing a relationship, so ask questions in order to get to know it. It is helpful to ask things like, "How are you trying to help me?" "How long have you been doing this job?" "How do you feel about the job you're doing?" Good relationships are reciprocal so it is important to notice how the part is responding to you as leader of the family. If you see an image of the part, notice if it is turned toward you. If not, notice the sensations associated with the part, and whether there is any shift when you make contact with it. Sometimes sensations will intensify when we first connect with a part. Now that it has your attention, it wants to make sure you don't turn away again. Ask yourself again, "Am I able to be with this part, just how it is, without needing it to change in any way?" If so, just be with it. Sometimes your presence is much more important than words. We do not want to interrogate our protectors; we want to befriend them. Friends hang out together. The pace of the conversation is not rushed; it is spacious.

The key question for any of our protectors is, "*What are you afraid would happen if you didn't do what you are doing?*" We do not want to ask this question too quickly because they might fear we have an agenda to make them stop doing something. After taking time getting to know a protector they have more trust in our genuine curiosity. At that point asking about their fears helps identify the exile it is protecting. Exploring a protector's fears is like peeling an onion. The first response to "What are you afraid would happen…" might or might not lead directly to an exile. If the protector says, "If I stop shutting down your sadness you will be overwhelmed by it" you can ask, "And what is your concern about that? What makes you think I can't handle being sad?" At that point the protector might show you a scene of an earlier time when you were experiencing significant grief. That is the exile it is protecting.

At this point in building your relationship with the protector it is helpful to validate their concerns. Express appreciation for how hard it has worked to protect you. It is also useful to update it; let it know that you are no longer the age of the exile. Any information about your adult capabilities and functioning can be helpful in differentiating your current situation from that of the exile. When the protector sees you as separate from the exile, you can let it know that at the right time, you intend to help the exile with the burden it carries from the experience of loss. Until then, see if the protector would be willing to allow you to lead in situations where you feel grief or are with someone else who is grieving. The protector can be present (and it will be!), but the goal is to see if it can be an advisor who might step in with a word of caution rather than being in charge and taking over.

Maintaining relationships with the protectors you identify and befriend will help them relax so you have more access to the healing resources you possess as an image-bearer when you or

Restoring Relationship

a loved one is in a season of loss. The resources of compassion, curiosity, and courage are particularly helpful. It takes courage to turn toward something as painful as grief. Curiosity can help us show genuine interest in another person's experience without bringing any agenda or advice about what they need to do. Compassion is the balm that helps us be with the emotions that deserve to be honored and attended to. Unblending from our protectors, differentiating ourselves as leader from the various family members, also makes space for more of the Spirit. When we ask a protector if they would be willing to allow us to breathe in more of the Spirit, they are more likely to be flexible and willing if we have a relationship with them. They will not give up their job until exiles are healed, but as we spend time with them and their trust grows, they are more willing to allow us to lead.

Your personal experience with loss will affect the degree to which you are able to independently connect with protectors associated with grief. If you have experienced significant and/or repeated losses, you might find that it will be difficult to unblend from protectors sufficiently to befriend them without the help of a therapist trained in the IFS model. However, the exercise of depicting the various parts that arise around grief can be a helpful first step in raising your awareness of the impact of loss in your life. It is validating to realize that the intensity of your response to circumstances makes sense. When there have been significant and repeated losses, your system will have many valiant protectors doing their best to help you function in spite of the burdens you carry. Your presence as leader, along with the presence of the Holy Spirit, builds the relationship they need in order for the journey of healing to begin.

Chapter Fifteen
The Agony of Betrayal

Monica's carefully constructed life was shattered the day she discovered her husband was having an affair. The first time we met she told me, "I chose him because he was safe." To find out that he was not safe – not trustworthy – turned everything she thought she knew about their relationship upside down. In over 20 years of marriage they had established a predictable routine; it wasn't exciting, but when she sometimes grew restless she thought, "At least he's safe." She knew what to expect from him and from their relationship.

Monica had no inkling anything was wrong until she inadvertently saw some of his text messages. Eventually she learned he had been having an affair for a year, lying to her the entire time and acting the way he always had during their safe and unexciting marriage. The impact of her discovery was devastating; not only did she learn that she had misplaced her trust in her husband, she no longer trusted herself.

Safety meant everything to Monica because she never experienced it as a child. Her father often left the family abruptly as he pursued numerous affairs. Her mother was preoccupied by the impact of her husband's infidelity and emotionally unavailable to her children. When her parents were together their fights were verbally violent, prompting her mother to frequently threaten to leave. In addition to living with emotional chaos, Monica rarely felt settled in school or with friends because the family moved frequently. Her childhood experiences left her feeling alone, unlovable, and not good enough. As a result, several protectors took on jobs to keep her vulnerability from surfacing. One was a hardworking manager who was diligent about school work and highly responsible as she launched her career. The protectors in her system kept her focused on things that were predictable and routine; fun just seemed too chaotic and risky.

Her husband was one of the first people she dated. He was several years older, established in a career, and a "gentleman." Monica said he was the first man she could trust, and the only man she knew who had never had affairs. Finally she had someone solid, stable, and trustworthy; she was no longer alone, no longer quite as convinced she was unlovable. Since our protectors constantly assess risk, they must have decided he was safe enough to trust because he didn't pose a threat to the most vulnerable parts of her inner family.

Then this safe person she chose so carefully – the person she had loved her whole adult life – betrayed the hope and trust she placed in him.

Betrayal comes in many forms, including abuse, intimate partner violence, infidelity and racism. The wounds carried as a result of betrayal are among the most complex and difficult to heal because betrayal shatters our hopes and expectations, violating the trust we placed in another person for our safety and wellbeing.

Trust is one of the cornerstones of interpersonal relationships. It is vital because it provides the confidence that the risk of vulnerability is worth taking. Any meaningful relationship involves vulnerability because intimacy requires a degree of openness that makes it possible to be wounded. So we rely on trust, on the degree of confidence we have in another person's trustworthiness, to provide sufficient safety to risk being vulnerable.

An individual's ability to trust is highly influenced by early life experiences. As we explored in Chapter Seven, infants seek proximity to caregivers so their needs can be met. Attuned and congruent responses from caregivers provide security, building a sense of trust that the world is safe. These early experiences form our expectations about relationships and impact the degree to which we are willing to place our trust in another person. For some, trust will be a life-long challenge as a result of early adverse experiences in relationships.

This is particularly true when someone is abused in childhood. Physical or sexual abuse and the neglect of a child's basic needs are obvious examples of a violation of a vulnerable child's most basic right to safety and protection. Less obvious, but equally devastating, is emotional abuse. Far too many children are exposed to verbal violence, degrading and shaming punishment, and more subtle but equally damaging comments that undermine their sense of self-worth. Often, children are subject to more than one type of abuse. Far too many of my clients were abused by a parent, either sexually or physically, and then endured years of shaming comments that conspired to convince them that they are unworthy and unlovable. Not only does the child who is abused struggle to trust another person, they do not trust themselves.

There is a terrible conflict in their inner family between the exile holding pain, protectors who work to suppress the pain, and a part who inevitably wants a loving relationship with the person who betrayed them. Because a child's survival depends on their primary caregivers, the child will often desperately pursue relationship – even with the parent who abused them. When a child seeks the love they deeply desire and deserve, another protector will often criticize them for it, becoming an inner "shamer" who echoes the shaming they experienced at the hands of their abuser. "You are so pathetic! Why do you keep trying to get him to love you?" This protector is sending the message that they should not trust themselves – they should not trust their own desire to be loved. It is a terrible dilemma, making trusting another person extremely challenging.

Child abuse is one form of the injustice of being deemed "less than" by someone in power. The ideal Jesus proclaimed is a kingdom in which everyone is invited to the banquet, equally loved and valued and worthy of a seat at the celebration. Sarah Bessey calls it the "kin-dom," highlighting the centrality of a fully inclusive community where there is no outsider.[127] Attitudes, policies, and practices that contribute to a hierarchy of human value are a betrayal of the Gospel. In Jesus' "kin-dom" there is "neither Jew nor Greek, slave nor free, male nor female" (Galatians 3:28). These were the categories that divided people in the early church. Over time, the categories have proliferated. Jesus knew our hearts; he knew our tendency to work to be on the "inside" where status confers safety and power. His actions and teaching challenged this protective impulse. Inclusive, lavish, even radical love should characterize the Christian community, if we are taking Jesus' example seriously. We betray *him* when we participate in any form of injustice that renders another human being "other."

Betrayal reverberates through our inner system, leaving heavy burdens. Distorted beliefs such as "I'm unlovable," "It's my fault," or "I'm unworthy" are common. Beliefs such as these provoke intense emotions including shame, terror, hopelessness, despair, and grief. Betrayal in adulthood will trigger earlier experiences, compounding the intensity of the impact of the more recent betrayal. As a result, protectors work feverishly, trying to restore order in the system. One strategy they employ is to ruminate about the event. If they can figure out "*Why did this happen?*" or "*What did I do wrong?*" they believe they can prevent betrayal in the future. Another strategy is hypervigilance – a protector who is always on alert to detect a threat. This is especially common with abuse or intimate partner violence, but can also occur following infidelity and other forms of betrayal such as racism. The "ping" of an incoming text message can send a person back to the moment they discovered the first suspicious message, throwing their system into a fight or flight response as the protector reacts to the threat. For others, the shame they feel can prompt protectors to distance and isolate, losing connection with caring people when they need it the most. Sometimes people notice a protector who constantly seeks validation of self-worth from others. The magnitude of the wound caused by betrayal can even lead to suicidal ideation.* The

---

* From an IFS perspective, thoughts of self-harm come from protectors who want to eliminate pain. When we connect with them, they typically say they will not have to harm the person if we can heal the pain. If you or someone you love is experiencing suicidal ideation call the National Suicide Prevention Lifeline at (800) 273-8255.

experience of betrayal is disorienting, chaotic, and exhausting. And that is just what is happening on the inside.

Betrayal also provokes myriad responses from people in our lives. With infidelity, family members and friends often choose sides, fracturing the network of support. In cases of abuse and intimate partner violence there is often involvement with social services and the legal system. Suddenly strangers are making decisions that – while in the service of safety – cause the hurting person to feel they are losing control of important decisions affecting their life. Intensely private matters are exposed publicly, in some cases even through the media. Individuals who experience racism often hear things such as, "I'm sure they didn't really mean that" or "You are being too sensitive," invalidating their experience.

The burdened exiles and hardworking protectors of the people closest to the person suffering from betrayal will also be impacted. As parts holding their own experiences of betrayal or difficulty trusting resonate with those of the betrayed, a variety of protective strategies will emerge. Evidence of protectors includes things such as ranting and raging at the person who broke trust, wanting to distance from the hurting person, feeling overly responsible for the hurting person, or jumping in with advice and problem-solving.

In the midst of the inner and outer chaos, confusion, and pain an agonizing question emerges: "Do I have to forgive?"

Scripture is clear about forgiveness. After teaching the Lord's Prayer to his followers Jesus expanded on one portion of it. "For if you forgive others when they sin against you, your heavenly Father will also forgive you. But if you do not forgive others their

Part IV – Loving Others as We Love Ourselves

sins, your Father will not forgive your sins"(Matthew 6:14-15, Mark 11:25).

Ouch. I want some wiggle room, but I am not finding any. When Peter asked – perhaps thinking he was going to impress Jesus with his generosity – "Lord, how many times shall I forgive my brother or sister who sins against me? Up to seven times?" Jesus again makes it clear that there should be no limit to our forgiveness of others (Matthew 18:21-35). He tells a story about a servant who owes a king "millions of dollars" and receives mercy; his staggering debt is canceled. We expect the man to do a happy dance, extolling the virtue of generosity. Instead, he attacks a fellow servant – who owes him a pittance compared to the sum he owed the king – demanding that it be repaid. His behavior is so shocking the distressed onlookers run to report this injustice to the king. The king says, "Shouldn't you have had mercy on your fellow servant just as I had on you?" The man's failure to extend mercy causes the king to withdraw his own. The king "handed him over to the jailers to be tortured, until he should pay back all he owed." And in case his followers did not get the point of the story, Jesus added, "This is how my heavenly Father will treat each of you unless you forgive a brother or sister from your heart."

Jesus uses hyperbole to get our attention. The message is clear; as his followers we are recipients of his forgiveness, and, motivated by gratitude and humility, we are to extend forgiveness to those who harm us. Despite the difficulty and complexity of forgiveness, we simply cannot dismiss it as unrealistic or impossible. If the answer to the question, "Do I have to forgive?" is *yes*, the next question is, "How – and when – do I forgive?"

When Scripture is as clear as it is on the topic of forgiveness, there can be a tendency to demand immediate forgiveness for ourselves and others. If a person who has experienced betrayal seeks support and prematurely hears, "You need to forgive," they will likely feel that their pain was dismissed. When our pain is invalidated we feel isolated and disconnected. Pressure to forgive quickly can also prompt the hurting person to think, "What's wrong with me that I can't forgive this person?" adding to their already considerable burdens. Exhorting someone to forgive without attending to their pain and without offering to walk with them on their journey of forgiveness breaks relationship when someone needs it most. Forgiveness is the outcome of a process – a process of connecting with protectors who shield us from the pain and then helping our wounded exiles release the burdens of betrayal. As McMinn wrote, "Forgiveness requires inner transformation."[128] Inner transformation happens as we lovingly connect with members of our inner family because in doing so we release constraints to the resources we possess as image-bearers. Forgiveness is a resource we already possess; it is fundamental to God's nature.

We miss the heart of forgiveness – the reason it is so vital – when we rush or force ourselves and others to forgive without engaging in a process of healing and transformation so that forgiveness can flow naturally. Jesus challenges us to forgive because the process transforms us, restoring relationship and helping us to live out the Great Commandment. Every time we are hurt by someone – or hurt someone else – we have the opportunity to choose the path of forgiveness, a path that first takes us inside to release the constraints to the compassion that will lead to forgiveness. "Be kind and compassionate to one another, forgiving each other, just as in Christ God forgave you" (Ephesians 4:32). Compassion is one of the resources we have as image-bearers and it is a *catalyst* for forgiveness. However, as we have explored, our protectors block our innate resources, and when we have been wounded by betrayal a time of healing is necessary to restore our leadership of the inner family, removing the constraints to our compassion so forgiveness is possible.

For the person suffering the effects of betrayal, the first step is to connect with the various protectors working to block the pain of the experience. The spiritual practice of establishing a relationship with a protector – unblending (differentiating yourself as leader from the member of the inner family), befriending it so you get to know its job and what it fears if it stops doing it, and allowing it to feel your interest and compassion for it – helps that protector begin to relax. Because there are likely to be many protectors this process can take time. Some of the protectors will be polarized with one another; they will have different ways of protecting you that cause them to be in a tug-of-war with each other. For example, one protector might want you to distance from people and another might want to pursue people to receive constant reassurance of your worth. Both protectors fear the same thing: the shame you now carry as a result of feeling unlovable. They are like warring family members, arguing over the best way to keep the shame from surfacing, so focused on one another and the risk of being overwhelmed that they have little or no connection with you as leader or with the Spirit. Patiently and persistently meeting with them will bring calm and more space for compassion. Ultimately, they will allow access to the hurting, vulnerable member of the family who needs healing.

Building relationships with our inner family members is the first step in the process of forgiveness. Our goal is to have an *intention* for relationship, but not a pressured time-bound agenda. An intention is open and patient, whereas an *agenda* has a timeline and feels more constrained. When we sense protectors have relaxed, and we have connected with the hurting parts to reassure them of our caring and compassion, we can do an experiment – bringing the person who betrayed us to mind and noticing what happens. If protectors have sufficient trust in our leadership, we will notice a shift in our perspective. We might have greater clarity about what led to a person's behavior, or we could notice having curiosity and a desire to gain more understanding. We might even notice feeling compassion as we recognize that they, too, have an inner family and the part of them that betrayed our trust is not all of who they are.

At this point you might be wondering if the process of forgiveness necessarily requires reconciliation with the person who betrayed you. Is it possible to forgive and to choose not to reconcile? Jesus' whole ministry is a continuous offer of reconciliation, and he empowers us to adopt that ministry as our own. In some cases, however, reconciliation might not mean a full restoration of relationship. Safety must be the first priority, and sometimes it is not safe to be in relationship with the person who inflicted harm. When a betrayal involves abuse or intimate partner violence, a rush toward full reconciliation of relationship is potentially dangerous. Both physical and emotional safety must be considered. One of the wounds of betrayal is a sense of powerlessness, so the individual who was harmed must feel free to choose the nature of the relationship, if any, they will have moving forward. Typically, both the betrayed and the offender must begin with their own healing before full reconciliation is possible. Healing makes it possible to see the betrayer as a fellow child of God whose actions do not represent their entire identity. The individual whose behavior caused harm is responsible for connecting with the parts who committed the egregious acts. Ultimately, they can connect with the wounded exiles in their inner family whose pain provoked their harmful actions. This individual work is all part of the ministry of reconciliation.

St. Francis of Assisi speaks to the recursive and relational nature of forgiveness – returning us to one of the reasons forgiveness is emphasized so clearly in Scripture. He said when friends "cause all manner of grief and trial...How can I suggest that you should greatly love such people?...For this reason: Their evil actions draw out and display to us our own evil responses – anger, gossip, slander, hatred and the like."[129] This is *not* to suggest parity between the actions of the abuser or the perpetrator or the unfaithful partner and whatever reaction the person who was betrayed feels in response. However, in this most grievous of injuries, our "tor-mentor"* teaches us where we need healing. The rage or hatred or impulse to be cruel that swamps my inner system as a result of being betrayed emerges because of the actions of the other person. I now have the opportunity to connect and build relationships with those fierce protectors and the very

---

*   Dr. Schwartz coined the term "tor-mentor" to describe someone whose behavior, while tormenting, teaches us something valuable when we turn inward and connect to our inner family members.

vulnerable exiles they shield. Every time I have a reaction to another person that is incongruent with my identity as a follower of Jesus I have an opportunity to make a "you-turn" – to turn my attention to my inner family to see who needs help. This is how we reconcile, how we live out the Great Commandment moment by moment, day by day – loving ourselves so we are better able to love God and one another.

****

Exercise
Befriending Protectors and Exiles Provoked by Betrayal

Recall a time when your trust was betrayed. If nothing comes to mind, consider whether someone ever made a commitment to care for you, or partner with you, and then violated that commitment. When you identify an example of betrayal, turn your attention inside and notice what's present. Some possibilities include:
- A *"minimizer"* – thoughts about not having experienced an egregious violation of trust or hearing, "Others had it worse."
- *Fear* – either a sensation in your body and/or a thought such as, "Why open that up? Leave well enough alone!"
- *Grief* over the loss of trust or loss of a relationship.
- *Anger* – the emotion and perhaps a related impulse to strike out verbally or physically.
- *Shame* – and perhaps a related belief of being unlovable.
- *Conflict* – parts who are polarized about whether to forgive.

Notice if you can be with whatever arises without needing it to be different, welcoming the inner family members that hold feelings, beliefs, and images of the incident or relationship. If there are many different parts present, it can help to externalize them by drawing each of them on a piece of paper or selecting objects that represent them. This allows you to unblend from them so you can help them get to know you as the leader of the family, offering resources such as curiosity, courage, calm, and compassion. Depending on how much time you have, you can select one of them – perhaps the one that seems most intense – and get to know it. If you have time to meet with more than one that's great, but you can also let them know you will return to them another time. You are building relationships with your inner family members so it is important to extend the same courtesy and respect to them as you would to any group of people vying for your time and attention.

The protectors you notice are on the job because of the burdens held by exiles. We always start by establishing a relationship with the protectors. There is so much benefit in getting to know them, and having them get to know you as the leader of the system. As they relax you might sense the presence of an exile. Our exiles are vulnerable; they hold distressing beliefs, emotions, images, and sensations. When you sense the presence of an exile, notice how you are feeling toward it. If there is any concern or fear about it, stay with the protectors. If your heart is open – you are curious, compassionate, welcoming – extend those qualities to it. Allow it to feel your gracious presence. Notice if there is any response. In this practice your presence as leader of the inner family – this new relationship – is the most powerful thing you can offer.

It is also important to either recall a situation, or imagine one, where someone who has suffered betrayal seeks your support. When you have something in mind, turn your attention inside and notice what is present. As always, you will want to be aware of thoughts, sensations, emotions, images, and impulses. What protectors arise in your inner system in response to another person's experience of betrayal? You might notice a desire to distance from the other person, being overwhelmed in the presence of their intense emotions, an impulse to give advice, or even a panicky thought such as, "What can I do! What should I say!" Just as your own exile needs your calm, confident and compassionate presence, the hurting parts of the other person need that presence as well. Connecting with your protectors helps them trust you enough to allow you to lead the interaction with the other person. Proactively doing this exercise can help you unblend more quickly when someone seeks your support. The goal is to offer the hurting person presence – connection that can begin to restore a sense of safety and trust.

Chapter Sixteen
A New Perspective on Addiction

I met an endearing young man who attended my church during a season when he was in town for a sober living program. When I told him I was working on this book, he generously allowed me to share his story. I chose to share the story in detail because it illustrates the complex variables contributing to addiction.

Justin remembers the day in second grade when the teacher told him he needed to go to the "special" reading group. There were three other groups in the class, but, due to undiagnosed dyslexia, he was not able to keep up in any of them. From an early age he was less verbal than his peers and when he did speak he stuttered. One of the girls in his class told him she didn't think he would graduate from elementary school.

Justin describes his two older sisters as "perfect." They participated in many extracurricular activities and excelled academically. Not only that, they were popular too. When Justin needed a tutor for help with reading, he knew he "didn't measure up." He recalls working really hard to memorize vocabulary words for a test in middle school and then being filled with anxiety and forgetting them the day of the test. His mother was mystified.

He did not seem to fit in a family where the expectation was that hard work equals positive results.

Athletics were easier for Justin, especially basketball, his favorite. All of the insecurity he felt in the classroom fell away on the court. His natural charisma and friendliness made him popular among teammates. His freshman year of high school things went pretty well on the court, but off the court he struggled academically and socially. He recalls procrastinating because school work was so difficult, and he became increasingly reserved socially. The summer after ninth grade he tried alcohol for the first time. He felt euphoric and began drinking regularly that autumn. He became "the life of the party" and loved being "in the spotlight." The anxiety he felt around girls melted away when he was drunk or high. His dream of finding "the" girl seemed to be within his grasp.

Then his parents saw some text messages and realized what was going on. Their understandable fear led to what felt to Justin like "constant punishment" and obsessive focus on his every move. Justin did not really have the words to explain what was going on for him. He felt alone, like he was the only teenager struggling academically and socially. He started believing what they said about him – that he was reckless and deserved punishment. He was afraid of the conflict he witnessed between his parents and feared he was ruining their marriage.

The stress was escalating, but basketball was still the one outlet he could count on. He was optimistic that he would make the junior varsity team, even though athletics were much more competitive in his large high school. Unfortunately, tryouts did not go well. He did not make the team, settling for being team manager so he could still participate in practice. He was miserable watching others play – feeling he had better skills – and when the players taunted him he lost his last healthy outlet for stress.

Justin reported that was the beginning of a downward spiral. He felt intense shame from others' judgment and the pain of social isolation. He pushed the limit at parties in a desperate attempt to get attention – craving validation and respect – but what was amusing to his peers at first became fodder for gossip. He recalls going to a party his junior year of high school and feeling everyone glaring at him. He was desperate to get high just to escape their judgment. He describes that period of his life as "unbearable." When he began treatment for substance abuse he said, "I didn't know who I was."

Take a moment and notice your response to Justin's story. What feelings does it evoke? What thoughts do you have? Is there any tension in your body?

Our response to Justin's story reflects our own experiences with addiction, those of loved ones, and the broader cultural messages about "addicts" and addiction. It is a complex topic – one about which we tend to harbor some pretty firm opinions. As you read the rest of this chapter, please ask parts of you who hold judgment or strong opinions if they would give you space to consider new information about addiction.

Fundamentally, "addiction is any repeated behavior, substance-related or not, in which a person [or what we would think of as a part of a person] feels compelled to persist, regardless of its negative impact on [their] life and the lives of others."[130] For purposes of clarity, I will use the term "addiction" in a broad sense, to include compulsive behaviors involving such things as gambling, pornography, food, exercise, work, etc. This is consistent with an important point: the key elements of any addictive or compulsive behavior are the same, whether it is a socially sanctioned activity such as work or exercise, or the use of hard drugs such as heroin. All addiction involves the following elements: "Compulsive engagement with the behavior, a preoccupation with it; impaired control over the behavior; persistence or relapse despite evidence of harm; and dissatisfaction, irritability or intense craving when the object – be it a drug, activity, or other goal – is not immediately available."[131]

Because it involves substances, Justin's story might fit the definition of addiction with which you are familiar. Consider Tom's story.

By mid-morning, Tom found himself looking forward to the moment the clock would read 1:00 p.m. That was the time he went to the gym. If he got a phone call right before one o'clock he felt irritated. He resented mandatory meetings scheduled for that time, and usually skipped them. Year after year he persisted in his "habit" of the midday workouts despite multiple orthopedic surgeries and sleeplessness related to pain. Workouts were the only time he was not preoccupied with job-related stress. He was in control at the gym; guys often commented on his physique and strength; it was his domain. Between the long workday and the extensive midday workout, he had little energy left in the evening for his family. If his wife expressed concerns, he quickly dismissed them, saying he "had no choice."

Tom's compulsive exercise meets all of the criteria for addiction. While substance abuse holds the greatest risk for health – and the potential for involvement with the criminal justice system – other compulsive behaviors can also be highly destructive to physical health, psychological well being, and relationships.

Why, then, are more and more people becoming addicted to substances and behaviors? Why are we seeing the proliferation of something that leads to so much suffering?

Because these strategies for numbing pain work – at least temporarily. As we have seen, our inner system is organized to protect us from pain – from the legacy of distressing experiences that resides within each of us. "A hurt is at the center of *all* addictive behaviors."[132] The nature and intensity of the hurt varies – ranging from trauma and abandonment, to beliefs about inadequacy and a sense of isolation, to the pressure to perform according to cultural norms. Just as the nature of the pain we carry lies on a continuum, so do the addictive behaviors used to numb that pain. For example, there is a strong correlation between early adverse experiences and substance abuse. Recall the Adverse Childhood Experiences (ACE) study we discussed in Chapter Nine. For each ACE "the risk of early initiation of substance abuse increased two to four times. Subjects with five or more ACE's had seven to ten times greater risk for substance abuse than did those with none."[133] The connection between adversity and addiction becomes clear when we understand addiction as a strategy for dealing with pain. "Drugs and other addictive practices offer a potent antidote to [distressing feelings]…That's why addiction so often follows psychological, social, or physical adversity in the early years of life."[134] When we see someone struggling with substance abuse, or any other harmful addiction, recognizing the underlying pain begins to open space for compassion and connection.

Restoring Relationship

Does the emphasis on pain as the reason for addiction surprise you? Traditionally, addiction was seen as a "moral failure." In more recent years we have typically been told that addiction is a "disease." While that shift has been somewhat helpful in reducing the shame associated with addiction, it is overly simplistic. "Viewing addiction as an illness, either acquired or inherited, narrows it down to a medical issue" and the disease model is simply not sufficient to explain addiction.[135] Scientists have not found a gene for alcoholism.[136] Whether we are talking about genes that predispose people to addiction or to any other physical and mental illness, researchers increasingly understand the interplay between our environment and the expression of genes.

What about the idea that people get addicted to substances simply because of the physiological effect of the substance? The primary evidence for this understanding of substance abuse was research done with rats.[137] The rats were put in cages alone and given the choice between water and bottles where the water contained drugs including cocaine and heroin. The rats compulsively drank from the drug-laced water; therefore, the drug was deemed addictive. One researcher wondered what would happen if rats were exposed to drugs when they were living in an environment that was more like paradise than solitary confinement. He conducted experiments where some rats were alone, and others lived in what he called "Rat Park." In Rat Park there were multiple rats, toys, a lot of space for running around – and two bottles, one with water and one with morphine – "an opiate that behaves just like heroin when it enters [rats'] brains."[138] The rats in isolation used high amounts of morphine but the ones in Rat Park used very little. This research demonstrates that "it isn't the drug that causes the harmful behavior – it's the environment."[139] "Addiction is an adaptation."[140] It is an adaptation to trauma, to adverse early experiences, to loneliness and isolation and a sense of meaninglessness – to disconnection from ourselves and others.

While it would be unethical to subject humans to the same experiment conducted with rats, we have evidence that the same phenomenon holds true for humans. A study documenting drug use among Vietnam vets noted that 20% of enlisted soldiers "met the criteria for the diagnosis of addiction while they were in Southeast Asia, whereas before they were shipped overseas fewer than one percent had been opiate addicts."[141] When they returned home the use of drugs "decreased to near or even below pre-service levels."[142] "These results suggested that the addiction did not arise from the heroin [or other drugs] itself but from the needs of the men who used the drug."[143]

Addiction is not moral failure. It is not genetic. Substance abuse is not an automatic effect of potent drugs. It is more helpful – and more hopeful – to understand that "the heart of addiction is dependency"[144] – dependency on a substance or behavior to numb pain, to soothe distress, to provide excitement, to mask boredom or hopelessness or despair. "Drugs…do not make anyone an addict, any more than food makes someone into a compulsive eater. There has to be a pre-existing vulnerability."[145]

There it is again: *vulnerability*.

As we have seen, the inescapable pain of life lived in a fallen world – and the vulnerability of the wounds we all carry – causes members of our inner family to take on protective roles. Our protectors always have a positive intention, no matter how dysfunctional their behavior might be. Under typical circumstances, when there is no major threat looming, our protectors are "helpers," maintaining harmony in our inner family. Some of our helpers are managers who proactively assist us with functioning well in our daily lives by helping us keep track of responsibilities and other necessary activities. In order to balance our highly responsible managers, our other helpers are "distractors" who remind us of the importance of comfort, rest, and recreation.[146] We can easily see how both managers and distractors have a positive intention, maintaining a balance of work and recreation.

When something happens to trigger our exiles, when pain surfaces, our protective helpers get much more polarized. If a distractor jumps in to numb the pain with a substance or behavior our managers are going to criticize to try to control the behavior. Imagine how a hard-working manager who diligently controls outward appearances feels when a distractor takes over and we drink to excess, perhaps in a public location where others notice our intoxication. Can you hear the criticism? Can you feel it in your body? What if drinking too much the night before means you are late to work or unprepared for an important meeting? Maybe your distractor likes to gamble. The rush of the risk and the possibility of winning keeps you at the table or the computer long after you gamble your budgeted amount. The savings account allocated for your child's college education is now empty. Harsh does not begin to describe what the inner critic – a manager trying to regain control of the situation – will sound and feel like in those circumstances. Now we are caught in a vicious cycle. The more we hear criticism, the more pain we feel, and the more imperative the substances or food or other distractions are to the protectors who want to suppress the pain.

Part IV – Loving Others as We Love Ourselves

Let's look at this cycle from the perspective of each of the parts – an exile, a distractor, and a manager.

The cycle begins with pain. We go to church or a social gathering and feel like an outsider. A child is struggling and we are swamped with hopelessness. The test comes back positive and the doctor's grim expression tells us the prognosis is not good. The demands of the job are relentless and the family is slipping away. The image in the mirror is horrifying. The pain of these circumstances can connect with the pain our exiles already hold, magnifying the impact. The intense emotions, the distressing beliefs, the images that run like a slideshow in our head, the tension that never seems to leave our chest or gut – the pain seems all-consuming.

Pain is the alarm bell for distractors. Remember, they are the firefighters who do not care if the hose destroys all the furniture; they have to put out the fire! They have tunnel vision, a single-minded determination to stop the pain. Consequences? They do not matter; the immediate danger is the pain. The shame, the sense of worthlessness, the intense anxiety or depression – however the pain manifests – prompts them to jump into action. They will use any strategy, no matter the fallout, to stuff the pain back down. Bingeing on food, drinking to excess, watching porn, piling up credit card debt by shopping – even thinking of ways to end a life that seems unbearable – all of these are strategies to distract from the pain. The protectors who react to pain are heroic in their own way, because they do what they deem necessary despite the cost.

And the managers make sure there is a cost. Our managers do not like chaos; they strive for order and control. They want us to be prepared, to look appropriate, to be on time. They want us to meet our responsibilities and they are very concerned about how others see us. Imagine how they feel when a distractor jumps in and hijacks our day with a compulsive behavior! The time spent engaging in those behaviors is time that is not spent on other responsibilities. A child is not picked up from school on time; a project is not completed by the deadline; we did the thing our spouse begged us not to do. Everything our managers have worked so hard to help us accomplish is lost – or so they think. In their frustration, these dedicated managers do what they believe is necessary to get our attention. They yell, they threaten, they point to people who think less of us because of our behavior. They shame us.

More shame, when we are already swamped with pain, means the distractors have to work even harder. Whatever behavior they use to try to numb the pain, they do more of it. And the frustrated managers? Now they are enraged. The criticism escalates. They threaten and point to all of the damage that is being done. More shame, more distraction, more criticism. It is a truly vicious cycle.

What can we do to disrupt this cycle?

As always, the way forward requires relationship. We start with the critical manager because their well-intentioned efforts are fueling the cycle. These managers are not well-liked by other parts of the system, so we will have to do as much reassuring as necessary to unblend from other parts and establish a one-to-one relationship. Imagine being the inner family member that is diligent and responsible and in control when the addictive behavior is anything but. These managers need compassion; they need a chance to air their grievances. They are intensely focused on consequences, and, often, their concerns are legitimate. Their jobs have been made much more difficult by the activity of distractors and they need to know that we understand their plight.

When the manager begins to trust us as leader of the inner family, we turn our attention to the distractor who engages in the destructive behavior. For perhaps the first time, we are offering to connect with them just as they are, without demanding change. Extending sincere curiosity opens a dialog. We can learn why they feel they have no choice about what they do – what they fear will happen if they stop doing it. They have an opportunity to share what it has been like for them to persevere despite the withering criticism of the manager. When they trust us they will show us the exile they are protecting, and the circumstances that prompted them to take on their job.

Having established relationships with both the managers and the distractors, we can now turn our attention to the exile(s) they protect. When addiction has been a strategy for dealing with pain for a long time, there can be multiple exiles. There is often a young part whose circumstances initially prompted the distractor to engage in an addictive behavior. Subsequent adversity, including the consequences of the behavior, can burden additional parts of the system.

The work with the members of the inner family involved with this cycle is complex and takes time. However, clients often experience a sense of relief and hope when they learn that there is a positive intention behind the behavior. They begin to understand that a part of them engages in a behavior for a reason. While it can be a powerful part that engages in destructive behavior, it is not *all* of them; their identity does not have to be reduced to the title "addict." Healing begins when they realize they still possess resources as the leader of the inner family. They begin to feel their confidence and courage as they unblend from fiercely critical managers and highly reactive distractors. They feel compassion for the vulnerable, burdened exiles, and hope for healing brings more calm to the whole system. They begin to believe that they are worthy of love.

Consider Justin's story from the perspective of exiles, distractors and managers. His early experiences in school burdened him with shame and the pain of being an outsider – both with peers and in his family. When academic and social pressure increased in high school he felt alone, an almost unbearable feeling at an age when feeling like an insider in peer groups is paramount. Isolation, combined with his increased awareness of the fact that he was not meeting family expectations for achievement, further burdened his system. Athletics initially served to distract him from the burdens, but when he did not make the team in high school his distractors had to find a more powerful way to numb the pain. Using alcohol and drugs not only helped him to escape the pain, he felt connected to people. He felt like part of the crowd – after all, everyone was experimenting with drugs and alcohol – instead of like an outsider. He took risks that got attention and much needed praise. Suddenly he was the person people gravitated toward – until he became the focus of whispers and glares and his parents fought about how to deal with him. Then the pain intensified and his managers echoed all of the external critics, condemning him, confirming his deepest fear that he was unworthy of love. His distractors reacted to numb the pain, consequences mounted, and finally, he found himself in treatment for substance abuse with "no idea who [he] was."

Justin's story helps us see the pain that builds up to the point where protective distractors feel they have no other choice but to engage in increasingly intense strategies. It also highlights the impact of both external and internal judgment – judgment inner and outer managers use to try to control distractors. It seems so necessary at the time, but it backfires, keeping a system locked in a vicious cycle of pain, distraction, criticism, and more pain. Breaking the cycle requires relationship. If we are going to be available to connect lovingly with our own parts struggling with addiction (and those of loved ones), we need to turn our attention inside.

****

Exercise
Connecting with Parts Involved with Addiction

It can be humbling to consider the ways we distract ourselves from the pain and stress of life. Unless we have struggled with an addiction, the tendency is to see someone whose distractors are destructive as "other." When we understand that we all need protective distraction at times, it helps us realize there is no "other;" there is just "us" – fellow humans doing the best they can to cope with pain.

What do your protectors do to distract you from stress? From pain?

Restoring Relationship

When you recognize a strategy employed by a distractor, turn toward it. Notice how you feel toward the part of you whose job it is to distract. It is very likely you will notice the presence of a critical manager. Turn your attention toward the manager. Notice how you feel toward it; is your heart open? Are you curious? Sometimes if your critical manager has been harsh other parts will be afraid of it. If it is difficult to want to connect with it, some compartmentalization can help. You can ask the manager to meet you in a separate room, allowing other parts to remain outside. (I realize this takes a bit of imagination! It helps to remember that our imagination is a powerful force for healing and connection.)

When you feel an open-hearted desire to connect with the manager ask it to tell you about the job it does for you.

- What prompts it to escalate the criticism?
- How does it feel about having to do that?
- What is it afraid would happen if it didn't?

Extend appreciation for its dedication and hard work. Then let it know that if you can connect with the distractor, the relationship you form with it will help it realize you are there to help with the pain, and it won't have to be so intense.

Turn your attention to the distractor. Notice how you feel toward it. Is your heart open? Are you curious? If there is any lingering judgment, ask the manager to give you more space. Reassure the manager that connection will calm the distractor. When you are able to accept the distractor just as it is, without needing it to change in any way, get to know it.

- Ask it to tell you what it is like to have to do the job it does.
- If it likes the job, ask what it likes about it. (Remember, distractors provide balance in our system; they might

view themselves as the fun-loving members of the family.)
- See if it will tell you when it started doing the job.
- If you are still open and curious, ask what it is afraid would happen if it stopped doing the job.

Our critical managers and our distractors tend to be polarized; the more intense the polarity – or tug-of-war – the more time we will need to spend meeting with each one of them for them to begin to relax. Critical managers do not trust the distractors to behave; they are very focused on the consequences of the distractor's behavior, and distractors are very focused on the pain. It takes persistence and patience to establish a relationship with them so they trust us to lead the inner family.

When both managers and distractors develop enough trust to allow us to lead, we can turn our attention to the vulnerable members of the family, the ones holding the burdens. We only want to take this step when we feel confident, compassionate, and open-hearted. There is no rush; we take as much time with the protectors as needed to gain their permission to connect with vulnerable exiles. Sometimes it will not be possible to take this step without the support of a therapist.

If you do feel compassion and an open-hearted desire to connect, turn toward the exile. When you begin to feel their tender emotions and their negative beliefs, when you see the scenes where distressing events occurred, let them know you are there. Spend time with them, always checking to make sure your heart is open. Let them feel your compassion. Notice how they respond to you. Patiently offer loving presence.

After getting acquainted with your own distractor, critical manager, and, if possible, the vulnerable ones they protect, think of someone you care about who struggles with addiction. Perhaps this is a person who has sought your support for their challenge. Maybe it is a leader you respected whose addiction ended their ministry. What do you notice? See if you can welcome the member(s) of your inner family who react to the person you brought to mind. Notice if you can be with them without an agenda to change them in any way. Focus on whoever seems to need your attention most. Extend curiosity; find out more about the job it does and what it fears would happen if it did not do the job. As you connect with parts that arise in response to the person they will calm and you will feel more space for grace. When this happens, bring the person to mind again. What do you notice now? Do you feel compassion for their struggle? Do you sense more courage about connecting with them in their pain? Do you feel more confident that relationship will be a balm to their wounds?

Addiction is one of the most complex challenges individuals and their families face. Working with protectors who are often entrenched in their roles and healing the underlying pain is not an easy or linear process. It takes a team – professionals, recovery groups, and individuals who are willing to work with their own reactions to addiction so they can remove the obstacles to their compassion, grace, and unconditional acceptance.

Chapter Seventeen
THE EMOTIONAL IMPACT OF PHYSICAL AND MENTAL ILLNESS

It had always been there, at least for as long as she could remember. The nausea, the tension in her body, the frustration about being fragile and the fear that the people she loved the most would get tired of her need for support. Days without anxiety were few and far between; sometimes it was there first thing in the morning and sometimes it blindsided her. Persistent nausea – her body's way of registering anxiety – made eating a chore and a source of distress. She became preoccupied with fear of the nausea. Sleepless nights filled with anxiety left her exhausted. She wondered if she would ever be free of it.

****

Ugh. Another day with an appointment, this time to see her therapist. It was bad enough that she had to take time to routinely go to the endocrinologist. Now her eating habits and weight gain were so concerning she had to see a dietician and a therapist. Constant worry about her blood sugar levels was impacting her ability to maintain a healthy diet. Sometimes she got so tired of eating healthy foods; when she was with friends she didn't want to be different! Other young adults could eat pizza and ice cream. It felt like she was wearing a sign saying, "I have diabetes!" How was she going to be able to live with this forever?

****

He was excited to be heading off to his parents' alma mater. The whole family looked forward to the years he would spend there, confident it would be the ideal foundation for his future. When his parents got the call that school administrators were concerned they were shocked. He hadn't been attending class. His roommate reported his poor hygiene and late night wanderings to the RA. When they spoke to him on the phone he didn't make sense. His hospitalization and diagnosis of schizophrenia was devastating.

****

Life was very, very good. All four children were launched, her husband was at the height of his career, and she was enjoying more time to pursue new interests. The nagging cough was annoying, so she decided to see her doctor. A diagnosis of stage IV lung cancer made no sense; surely they were wrong! She'd never smoked and had always been active and healthy. She gathered with friends for prayer each week through the months of surgery, chemotherapy, various medications, and planning her daughter's wedding. About a year and a half after diagnosis she learned the cancer had spread to her liver and she decided not to have additional chemotherapy. She wanted to preserve her strength for her daughter's wedding, and she knew the chemo would not cure the disease. The wedding was held the week after the family gathered for her memorial service.

****

Pause and notice your response to these stories of mental and physical illness. What sensations do you feel in your body? Is your mind filled with images and thoughts about your own family and friends and their trials? Would you like to just shut the book and distract yourself? Are there tears as you feel the weight of the suffering of these people you do not even know?

It can be difficult to read about the impact of illness on people's lives – our signal that if we are going to be able to support someone in a time of illness we have some work to do. I could have shared so many more stories, and I considered doing so because I want you to connect with the emotional impact of illness. I realize you might be well aware of the toll it takes on others, especially if you are in a position where you have accompanied many people on the journey through the "valley of the shadow of death." My hope is that you will connect with your own emotional response to illness. As much as any challenge we face in life, illness stirs up deep-seated needs and beliefs, it confronts us with vulnerability in its many forms, and it provokes our protective team.

Why would illness be a particularly challenging topic? After all, we hear about people who are ill all the time. On a given Sunday approximately 75% of the prayer requests at my church are for people who are ill. Yet, illness is not what we *expect* in life. We expect to be healthy. We expect to have control. We expect a happy ending. One of my first psychotherapy mentors said our

Restoring Relationship

expectations are one of the biggest drivers of distress. We have all sorts of expectations for relationships, for our children, for our wellbeing. Most of us expect to wake up healthy and energetic and able to tackle whatever awaits us each day.

I am writing this chapter in the midst of the coronavirus pandemic. The pandemic has challenged so many assumptions and expectations, whether we were aware of them or not. I doubt many – outside of the infectious disease professionals – would have ever thought we would all be house-bound for weeks – let alone months – at risk of contracting a deadly virus for which there is currently no treatment and no vaccine. Stories of seemingly healthy people on ventilators fighting for their life surrounded by heroic medical professionals in protective gear that looks like something out of a sci-fi movie leaves us speechless and in tears as the death toll mounts. Countless families face threats well beyond the possibility of infection. Unemployment is rising at dizzying rates. Food banks are trying to meet unprecedented demand. Children are more exposed to adverse childhood experiences such as financial insecurity and rising domestic violence that can lead to a life-long risk for mental and physical illness. The elderly, isolated from loved ones, are at high risk for depression – and many have died alone. In some cities, doctors express concern that people with other conditions will avoid seeking medical care, potentially worsening their outcome. The ripple effect of the pandemic will be felt for years, and we might never fully measure the impact on mental and physical health.

This is *not* what we expected when we celebrated the start of a new year. We did not expect a tidal wave of vulnerability.

As the devastating impact of the pandemic was becoming obvious, we entered Holy Week – a Holy Week unlike any other. Many spiritual leaders reflected on aspects of Holy Week that typically get less attention, such as Holy Saturday – the day after the crucifixion – a day of despair, of intense fear of the unknown, of deep grief. Jesus' followers had no idea that the tomb would be empty the next day, let alone that they would dine again with Jesus. They just huddled together in what was, perhaps, the most vulnerable time of their life. Illness can feel like Holy Saturday. There are often unknowns – about treatment, about prognosis, about what the future looks like. The initial shock makes it difficult to process the new reality. There is often confusion and deep disappointment. We feel isolated and lonely even when family and friends are near; it can feel like no one else fully understands the experience. Illness confronts us head on with vulnerability in all its forms – including fear, powerlessness, pain, weakness, and hopelessness.

I, too, had a different Holy Week than I expected. I was diagnosed with breast cancer.

When the surgeon called with the results of the biopsy and I heard the word "carcinoma" I was surprised, despite tests that indicated this was a possibility. Even some of the doctors led me to believe it was probably "nothing." I had a, "Wait…what??" moment and had to ask the surgeon to slow down a bit. Another surgery and more referrals to specialists? It was a lot to absorb.

As I shared the news with my family I noticed how difficult it was to allow myself to feel the grief. I was not afraid (yet), but I was sad. The sadness would well up, particularly when I spoke of the diagnosis and the treatment required, and I would find myself shifting to expressing gratitude for the wonderful health-care I was receiving and for an excellent prognosis. My gratitude was sincere, but it was also protective. Sadness is vulnerable, and shifting to gratitude tamps it down. The challenge is to allow *all* of our emotions the space they deserve. It became more important than ever to prioritize the daily practice of attending to my inner family. Even during the best of times this practice is essential, partly because my managers are really good at what they do. They keep me on task, they are committed to fulfilling responsibilities, and they assess each day to make sure I am "productive." They have a tendency to take the lead. I had to negotiate with them, acknowledging and appreciating the terrific job they do, so they would relax and allow me to be "productive" in a different way – by listening to what my vulnerable parts needed and offering them the tenderness they deserved.

I was also very aware of a protector who let me know that it is *not* ok to "need attention." I felt conflict between parts of me any time I shared the news – between the one who did not like what it identified as "seeking attention" and the natural impulse to share something important, to connect with my loved ones to receive comfort. Loving relationship is our greatest need, yet it feels risky. It is risky to be exposed as having a need, rather than being the person who can meet a need. I know I feel more in control, more powerful, (can you feel that protective energy?) when I am tending to someone else's needs than when I am allowing someone to tend to mine. What if I express a need and it is not met? That is the risk. And all of us have had that experience. The degree of risk depends on our history, especially the nature of our relationship with our primary caregivers. For some, trusting another person to meet a need is extremely difficult. Typically, the word "needy" is pejorative; it is an insult. But when we are ill, we *are* needy – we need comfort, compassion, and connection. We need space to allow the impact of the illness to surface, so all parts can be met with tenderness. Protectors rush in and take up all of the space, so we must start by welcoming them and appreciating how they are trying to help us. When the protector who was concerned with my neediness was met with comforting compassion it relaxed and allowed me to receive the connection I needed.

My minimizer was also on the job from the moment I received the diagnosis. Minimizers – protective parts that downplay our experience – are very common. They assess our experience, compare it to what others are going through, and send the message that we really should not pay attention to our own situation. Receiving my diagnosis in the midst of a pandemic where so many were suffering really gave my minimizers some ammunition. Our minimizers not only want to shield us from vulnerable emotions; they are also very aware of what others say. I could tell that my minimizer was responding, at least in part, to what it heard from others. "Oh well, it is what it is." "I'm sorry, but at least they caught it early." "You seem great." My minimizer colluded with the minimizers in other people's inner families in a group effort to avoid sitting in the silence, to avoid sitting with the grief, to avoid the tenderness of a schedule that was suddenly full of surgery, oncology appointments, and radiation treatment.

Minimizers block curiosity. They jump in with statements. Curiosity fosters relationship through questions. *"How are you? What do you need?"* Our minimizers want to help us in the only way they know how. They seem to think giving attention to our own needs means we are not acknowledging others' needs. But this is not a zero sum game. The more we practice gracious acceptance of our own needs, the more adept we are at extending the same grace to others. Connecting with our minimizers leads to the vulnerability they fear. They calm down when they trust us, as the leader of the inner family, to be able to navigate our vulnerability with innate resources such as courage, confidence, and compassion. When they relax we have more space for grace, for acceptance of the struggle so we can be with it just as it is in the moment with no pressure for it to be other than it is.

My protectors did their jobs well during the day. Fear only showed up at night. I have never had much difficulty sleeping, but the first few nights after receiving the diagnosis I was restless, waking up with questions, processing this new reality. Information helped me the most with fear. As I met with the various doctors on my treatment team I felt increasingly confident. Information often helps the protectors with the fears they hold. As we focus on them and build a relationship with them and learn about their fears we can update them with new information. We will often notice that they ease and we feel more calm.

The challenge with information is *timing*. If we rush to give someone information about their illness without making space for their emotional response, the information will not be helpful. The person can feel dismissed or lonely or wrong for feeling whatever they are feeling. It is also helpful to be aware of our motive in offering information – to ask ourselves whether we are uncomfortable just being present with someone in their grief and fear. It is a good practice to ask if the person would like to hear any information you have to offer. The emotional storm following a diagnosis, or a setback, or the despair of long weeks, months, and years with no recovery makes it difficult to absorb information. We also need to be mindful of the difference between information and advice. As Philip Yancey writes in his wonderful book *Disappointment with God*, "The Book of Job plainly shows that…advice does nothing to answer the questions of the person in pain."[147] In order to connect in a loving way, we need to meet the person where they are – without needing them to change in any way – bringing compassion and a calm willingness to be with them on their journey.

My condition is acute; while I will be on medication for several years, the majority of treatment and symptoms will resolve within a few months. Many people have chronic conditions, one of the myriad physical or mental health issues with no cure and life-long effects. Some of the protective responses will be the same, but there will be other strategies and, perhaps, greater vulnerability. I have found that clients with chronic conditions often have a hypervigilant protector who is always on alert for symptoms. These extremely hard-working protectors scan to detect evidence of symptoms so other parts of the system can jump into action to manage distress on difficult days. There can be a team of protectors who have jobs related to coping with the illness, which can be both helpful and can also block compassionate connection with the hurting parts of the inner family. I have encountered angry protectors who are incensed about the injustice of the illness. They, too, are blocking vulnerable ones who hold despair, hopelessness, and doubts about God's love for them. Those feelings make sense because illness *is* unfair and unjust. We have a deep sense of the injustice of it. It is a stark reminder that all of Creation is "groaning," in "bondage to decay," waiting for the "freedom and glory" that is God's will for his creation (Romans 8:20-22). "We need a new heaven and a new earth, and until we have those, unfairness will not disappear…The Cross of Christ may have overcome evil, but it did not overcome unfairness."[148] The crucifixion was the greatest injustice, the greatest unfairness, and the greatest proof that, "because of Jesus, God understands how [we] feel."[149] There are few things more comforting than the confirmation that our feelings are valid. This is a gift we can offer one another.

Many of us have protectors who work hard to figure out, "*Why?*" This protector is often connected to an exile holding a painful belief that they did something to deserve their illness – that it is a reflection of their unworthiness to enjoy the abundant life others seem to take for granted. The protector believes that if it can find an objective, factual reason for the illness it mitigates the possibility that they somehow merit their condition – it blocks the vulnerability of the painful questions of, "Why me?" and "Why are others healed and I'm not?"

The desire to figure out "why?" can lead to an effort to make sense of a situation from a spiritual perspective. I have repeatedly heard some version of "God won't give you more than you can handle," a misquotation – and misunderstanding – of 1 Corinthians 10:13. The verse actually reads, "No temptation has overtaken you except what is common to us all. And God is faithful; he will not let you be tempted beyond what you can bear. But when you are tempted, he will also provide a way out so that you can endure it." The context of this verse – which says nothing about God "giving us" trials – is a warning against idolatry.[150] The Corinthians were being warned not to trade the freedom they had in Christ for some form of idolatry.[151] When this verse is plucked out of its context and shared with someone who is suffering it implies that God chose them to receive their suffering, and that their suffering has been deemed bearable by God. The reality is that people routinely experience overwhelming distress. That is difficult to accept; our protectors do not like the vulnerability of "senseless" suffering. They want to make sense of it, to find the reason for it. We can feel protective energy in other common attempts to spiritualize distress, including asserting that God is "testing" the person or that this must be part of God's plan for them. Imagine how you would feel if you had just received a difficult diagnosis, or if you were (or are) dealing with a chronic condition and you heard these assertions about God "giving you" the illness, or testing you, or including this in his plan for you. Do you feel comforted? Do you feel loving compassion? I certainly would not. It helps to remember that God was angry with Job's friends – who offered just about every reason for Job's suffering that you can imagine – telling them, "you have not spoken of me what is right" (Job 42:7). We simply do not have God's perspective, we do not have all of the information, and we almost never know "why" someone has the illness they do.

Rather than misapplying or misquoting Scripture and adding to a person's burdens, we need to offer ourselves as companions on the journey. As Jesus prepared his disciples for his departure his emphasis was on relationship. "Abide in me" (John 15:4). "I will not leave you as orphans…" (John 14:18). "Love each other as I have loved you" (John 15:12). He repeatedly tells them about the Spirit – an "advocate" to help them and be with them forever (John 14:16). "The Spirit will not remove all disappointment with God. The very titles given to the Spirit – Intercessor, Helper, Counselor, Comforter – imply there will be problems."[152] We do not have to twist Scripture to make sense of suffering. As Yancey says, "…if I ever wonder about the appropriate 'spiritual' response to pain and suffering, I can note how Jesus responded to his own: with fear and trembling, with loud cries and tears."[153] He asked his closest friends to be with him when his "soul [was] overwhelmed with sorrow to the point of death" (Matthew 26:38). Even Jesus needed relationship. Whatever the course of illness – whether physical or mental illness, whether acute or chronic – we need loving relationships with our inner family, with Jesus, and with the family and friends who can meet us where we are with gracious acceptance.

The message to the Corinthians *was* not that God will not give you more than you can handle. The message was, "we have one hope: the faithfulness of God. God is trustworthy, and even if the situation seems impossible, nothing is beyond God's power and grace."[154] Illness – like any season of distress – presents an opportunity to move beyond a relationship where we trust God only if our expectations are met to one that "transcends any hardship."[155] The more we cultivate relationship with God, one another, and with our inner family, the more we build the relationships that sustain us through trials. When our dedicated protectors rush in to help with the toll illness takes, they need our attention; they need us to open space for more of God's power and grace. And in connecting with the vulnerable parts of our system that carry our deepest needs and pain, we can live out the promise that nothing "in all creation will be able to separate us from the love of God that is in Christ Jesus our Lord" (Romans 8:39).

****

Exercise
Connecting with Our Response to Illness

What do you notice after reading this chapter? Turn your attention inside. Who is present? Do you have a protector like one of the ones I described? Whatever your personal response to illness – your own or others' – it is likely there is some evidence of a desire to protect yourself from the impact.

When you identify one of your protectors, notice whether you would like to get to know it. Is your heart open? Are you curious? If not, invite any parts who are blocking your connection to step back. They do not have to go far; if they need time with you, let them know you will be with them when it is their turn. If there is a strong reaction to the first part and it is not easing, turn your attention to the one having the strongest reaction.

After you identify the member of your inner family you want to connect with, notice how it shows up. What do you feel in your body? Are there thoughts? Is there an image? What emotions are present? As you focus on it, ask yourself again if you are open to connecting with it. When you are curious, ask what this part would like to share with you. You might hear from it, you might get more sensation or emotion, or you could see other images. Just be with whatever arises. Can you send appreciation to this dedicated member of your inner family? If so, notice the response to your appreciation. Feel free to ask more questions: How long has it had this job? What does it hope will happen? What is it afraid would happen if it did not do its job?

Our protectors are fear-driven. They do what they do out of fear, and illness provokes a lot of fear. We fear the loss of control, the unknown, the emotional and physical pain, the loneliness. When your protector trusts you enough to show you what it fears, it is important to check your heart to see whether you are open to connecting with the vulnerable one(s). Do you feel compassion, courage, or confidence? If so, just be with the tenderness, however it is manifesting. Allow it to feel your gentle, comforting presence. Notice how it responds to you. Breathe in more of the Spirit; bring more of God's mercy to this hurting part of you.

It is important to get to know the protectors who arise as a result of your own illness, and those who do their jobs as a reaction to illness in others. Sometimes they will be the same, but they might be different. They might be connected to the same vulnerable exiles, but they might not be. I encourage you to explore what arises any time you are confronted by illness. No matter the diagnosis, your faithfulness in connecting with your inner family members will enable you to accompany others with the compassion that heals.

Chapter Eighteen
FROM EXHORTATION TO TRANSFORMATION

Our mission is clear. As Jesus prepared his followers to carry on his earthly ministry he said, "Love each other as I have loved you" (John 15:12). Love takes many forms as we seek to meet the needs we encounter. When we are in a season of distress, whatever form our distress takes, the greatest need is for love expressed through relationship. Open-hearted relationship allows us to offer presence and bear witness, drawing upon the resources we possess as image-bearers filled with the Spirit. This relationship is sacred ground where tender, vulnerable, hurting souls receive healing. It is a beautiful and compelling mission, but it is not easy.

Fulfilling our mission requires more than exhortation. It requires transformation.

Transformation is not required because we *lack* something, such as compassion. Being made in God's image means that we already have all that we need for loving relationships with God, one another, and ourselves. But those resources are blocked; they are constrained by the burdens we carry because we are inherently vulnerable.

Being made in God's image includes being vulnerable; just as God's heart can be broken, so can ours. We risk the possibility of being wounded *simply by having needs*. From the moment we are born we need attuned connection to feel secure and to learn to trust. We need to know that what we feel is valid, and we need connection that is safe enough to express our feelings. We need to know we are worthy of love simply because we exist. Inevitably, some of these needs are not met. There is no perfect parent and all of us are embedded in a complex web of circumstances and relationships that fall short – sometimes egregiously short – of an ideal environment for growth. When important needs are not met, we take on burdens: distorted beliefs, painful emotions, distressing images, and uncomfortable sensations. We hold the burdens from difficult experiences in neural networks, and we are primed to recall them as a way of ensuring survival.

With the God-given gift of imagination, when we turn our attention to these painful places and intentionally "light up" the neural networks that hold them, we find that burdens are held by members of our inner family who are often very young. When we are young, we are susceptible to making meaning of adverse circumstances by placing blame on ourselves. We decide we are defective: bad, unlovable, unworthy. Even if we are too young to articulate the beliefs, we hold the pain of shame, grief, and terror that accompany the sense that we are at fault for what we experience.

Picture a very young child weighed down by painful emotions. Imagine that child believing in their own culpability for something you can readily see could never have been their responsibility. Do you feel the injustice? Do you grieve the loss of

Part IV – Loving Others as We Love Ourselves

innocence? Do you have compassion for their distress? *That* is the loving relationship they need but is often blocked.

The vulnerability they carry is risky and potentially overwhelming. Out of fear, other members of the inner family adopt strategies to either avoid being overwhelmed, or to numb and distract when the pain surfaces. All of our hard-working protectors mean well; they have a positive intention. But strategies rooted in fear do a lot of harm. The problematic approaches for handling distress that we surveyed in Part I are all examples of the influence of protectors who, generally, mean well but who block loving relationship. When we become aware of our own judgment or legalism, it is a clue that there is a rigid protector who is often working to help us feel we are on the "inside," that we are superior in some way to the other person. We do not struggle with their issue; we know the "right" way to live. This protective strategy blocks the pain of being an outsider, one of the most difficult things we experience. Or, when we find ourselves rushing to give advice, to tell others how to resolve a dilemma or to move on from a difficult situation, we know a protector is doing their job, blocking our discomfort (and blocking our hearts). And when we approach distress with the assertion that a person's beliefs are the problem, rather than having curiosity about why they hold those beliefs, protectors are in the lead, exiling the part holding the distressing beliefs.

Just as vulnerability is inevitable, so are protective strategies. We all have exiles, and we all have protectors. The burdens our protectors and exiles carry block the resources we possess as image-bearers. They take up space meant for the Spirit. They take over leadership of our inner family, blocking our freedom to love freely and unconditionally. We cannot fulfill our purpose as followers of Jesus without engaging in a process of healing.

Our purpose is clear: God calls us to love God, one another, and ourselves. Loving in a way that fulfills the promise of Jesus' ministry requires us to intentionally engage in the process of transformation. As the first followers of Jesus fanned out to carry on the ministry of love, the Apostle Paul repeatedly wrote about the importance of transformation. "...I urge you to live a life worthy of the calling you have received" (Ephesians 4:1). "Do not be conformed to this world, but be transformed by the renewing of your mind" (Romans 12:2). Our minds are more than thoughts; our minds are shaped in relationship and through emotion. Paul urges, "Therefore if you have any encouragement from being united with Christ, if any comfort from his love, if any common sharing in the Spirit, if any tenderness and compassion, then make my joy complete by being like-minded, having the same love, being one in spirit and of one mind" (Philippians 2:1-2).

Transformation is the process that releases the constraints to our love, to all of the resources we possess as image-bearers. It is the process that heals our pain. Richard Rohr writes, "Spirituality is always eventually about what you do with your pain...If we do not transform our pain, we will always transmit it."[156] We transmit our pain when protectors lead our inner family. And we transmit our pain when burdened exiles flood our system, wreaking havoc in our lives. In order to transform our pain we must connect with our fear-driven protectors and our vulnerable exiles. Building relationships establishes trust and safety so wounds can heal. As healing happens, more of our intrinsic resources are available. We are increasingly able to lead our inner family, drawing on resources such as compassion, curiosity, and clarity. And we have a more spacious soul – more room for the Spirit.

What do your circumstances require? What resources do you need to draw upon? You possess them. You are made in God's image and you can invite more of the Spirit to strengthen your relationship with the inner family members whose burdens block your innate resources. Relationships develop over time. Your goals, your calling, and your purpose in this moment deserve the time it takes to foster relationships with your inner family members. Committing to this new spiritual practice, to a new means of transformation, allows you to access what you need, no matter the challenge you face.

We do not engage in the work of transformation solely for ourselves. God calls us to this journey of healing so that we can participate in God's plan of redemption. Each time a hurting person is met with loving relationship redemption happens. Their pain is transformed through loving connection. In these moments, we participate in the ministry Jesus proclaimed (Luke 4:18-19). We partner with him in bringing freedom to prisoners, the exiles who have been locked away. We engage with him in restoring sight to our blind inner family members, the protectors whose fear limits their perspective and locks them in a rigid pattern of behavior.

Transformation is possible. Healing is possible. Jesus showed us the possibilities during his earthly ministry and then empowered us to carry on the ministry "to the ends of the earth" (Acts 1:8). The new spiritual practice facilitates healing and transformation. It enables us to manifest the image of God more fully, to be in harmony with the Holy Spirit, and to restore the loving relationships for which we were created.

Appendix A
RESTORING RELATIONSHIP: A NEW SPIRITUAL PRACTICE

Loving God, one another, and ourselves requires commitment to transformation. As with any transformative spiritual discipline such as prayer, worship, and service, routinely engaging in the practice is necessary for healing and growth. Good relationships require attention. In order to build relationships with our inner family members it is important to be intentional about connecting with them. This spiritual practice is a step-by-step guide to support that process. In doing so, we will find that we are increasingly able to have the kind of loving relationships with one another and God that are at the heart of our faith.

It is helpful to keep the guiding principles for building relationships in mind. As image-bearers, we have intrinsic resources that cannot be damaged by life experiences. Rather than developing something we lack, our focus is on *releasing constraints* to what is already there. The resources include the eight "C's":

- Curiosity
- Calm
- Compassion
- Connection

- Clarity
- Confidence
- Courage
- Creativity

The resources also include the five "P's":
- Patience
- Persistence
- Presence
- Playfulness
- Perspective

Added to these resources are the qualities representing the Spirit's presence such as love, joy, and gentleness. Restoring relationships with inner family members who have lacked access to the leader of the family releases these resources, transforming fear and pain, and opening space for love and grace.

Preparation

Select a quiet place. The less noise in your outer environment, the easier it will be to focus on your inner world. As you quiet yourself, take a few slow, deep breaths. As you breathe in, imagine taking in more of the Spirit. You can add a prayer or recite verses that are meaningful for creating this sacred space. "Be still, and know that I am God" is a personal favorite (Psalm 46:10). In the Psalm, God urges the psalmist to embrace stillness in a context of chaos. It is a reminder that, whatever your circumstances, it is possible with God's help to make the space for relationship with your inner family members. You might want to imagine a meeting place that is ideal for connecting with your inner family members. The space you create with your breath allows just the right distance for good connection.

Inner Awareness

Now turn your attention inside, taking time to notice thoughts, emotions, images, and sensations. These are held by members of your inner family. Allow your breath to be a calming reminder of the presence of God.

Focus

Focus on whatever is most present or intense. You can also ask, "Who needs my attention right now?" Notice whether you are open to connecting with it, and if you are curious to learn more about why it is there. Often, more than one part will be present simultaneously, which can block your curiosity. Start by asking if other parts would be willing to give you some space so you can connect with the one who most needs your attention.

Unblending

Sometimes there are many parts present at the same time, or, there can be one that has a lot of energy. As a result, you will notice that you do not feel separate from the part or parts. For example, if you are feeling highly anxious, it might feel like, "That's me. I'm anxious." The premise is that, no matter how intense a part is, unless you notice the qualities of the leader of the system, it is a part. The leader of the family draws on intrinsic resources (such as the eight C's and five P's I mentioned above) and the power of the Holy Spirit. When these qualities are absent, "unblending" – differentiating between parts of the inner family and the leader of the family – is necessary. Remember, the goal is to establish a relationship between the leader of the family and the individual family members. To determine whether you, the leader, are blended with other parts, ask *"Am I able to be with this part of me without needing it to change in any way?"* If the answer is no (if there is fear, criticism, distractedness, or any other reaction) ask the inner family members holding those reactions to give you space. In order to befriend a particular part, it is necessary to unblend from other parts. Generally, parts will be willing to step back and wait their turn. If not, a persistent part who does not seem to want to allow you to focus on the original part will need your attention first.

Externalizing

Helpful in unblending, externalizing involves depicting inner family members through art, using objects, etc. For example, a "parts map" depicts each member of the family that arises in response to a situation. Parts can be represented on paper as shapes, colors, and words, and their connection to one another and to the leader of the system can also be illustrated. Objects representing the parts can be used to create a scene depicting your inner family. As you externalize parts, notice if you feel more spacious, open, and calm about connecting with them.

Befriending

Now that you have identified a part needing attention, you are ready to build a relationship. It is helpful to remind yourself that this is no different than developing any other relationship! It involves listening, being open and curious, and allowing your love to create a gracious space for connection. Curiosity is key, because it will prompt questions that help you learn the part's intention for the system. *How is it trying to help you? How does it feel about the job it has to do? What is it afraid would happen if it didn't do it?* Notice the response to your questions. Sometimes there will be silence or even a snarky, "Well it's about time you noticed me!" It can take time to build trust, so extending compassion without words or questions is valuable. Appreciation is balm for our parts. Let the hard-working members of your inner family know that you are grateful for their dedication. Other parts might creep back in, so sometimes it helps to ask them if they would be more comfortable going elsewhere, such as into another room, while you connect with the first part.

Updating

Providing information during the befriending process deepens relationships with your inner family members. They are typically stuck in the past, either at the time where a protector took on its job, or at the time when an exile became burdened with distress. As a result, they do not know the adult who leads the family. Information about your adult context and functioning builds trust in your capabilities. It is particularly helpful to share the resources you possess as an image-bearer. In addition, reminding inner family members about the presence of the Spirit and the qualities the Spirit brings (love, patience, kindness, gentleness, etc.) inspires confidence that you can be trusted to lead the inner family. It is not unusual for members of the inner family to doubt that you possess these resources. They have been cut off from them. If there is a lack of confidence about the resources, that simply means a part is blocking it. Unblending from that part will open up more confidence.

Connecting with Others

Often the part needing your attention is having a response to an important person in your life. The reactions we have to other people are clues about where we need healing. For example, you might notice disappointment or frustration when you turn your attention inside. As you connect with the inner family member holding the emotion, you learn that someone said or did something that provoked the feelings. After you connect with the part and it trusts you to lead, you are ready to turn your attention to the person who initially provoked the response. As a result of unblending and befriending, qualities such as calm and confidence facilitate a receptive connection with the other person.

Appendix B
GLOSSARY OF KEY TERMS

Befriending: Establishing a relationship between the leader of the family and a member of the inner family. Relationships are reciprocal, so this process involves being curious about a particular part's role and experience, as well as noticing how the part responds to your presence and interest.

Blending: When members of the inner family react to circumstances they move into the space occupied by the leader of the family. They block the resources we possess as image-bearers, and they block the presence of the Spirit. Picture a room where you are sitting with members of your inner family. Everyone is calm until circumstances arise that cause some of the family members concern. They raise their voices, jump out of their chairs gesturing, and they are unresponsive to your initial request to slow down so you can listen to each of them. It can feel like the leader has lost influence over the system.

Burdens: Distressing, adverse, and traumatic experiences leave their mark on our inner family members. The neural networks formed as a result of these experiences hold beliefs, emotions, images, and sensations, all of which become a strain on the inner system. As with heavy baggage, burdens constrain a part's inherent resources, keeping them from thriving and making their unique contribution to the system. Connecting with parts helps them release their burdens.

Exiles: Members of the inner family who hold burdens from distressing experiences. Their burdens include distorted beliefs such as, "I'm unlovable," or "I'm unworthy"; painful emotions such as grief, shame, and terror; distressing images from scenes where they experienced adversity; and sensations associated with their negative experiences. Because of their painful burdens, they are suppressed, or "exiled," by the protective members of the inner family.

Externalizing: When we are blended with several parts it can help to have a tangible representation of each of them. Drawing a part (whether you are an artist or not!) or using an object to represent it helps with the process of unblending. One helpful technique is a "parts map" where each part that surfaces in response to a particular issue is depicted. As you draw each part (such as a blob with a color matching the part's energy), you can notice its proximity to other parts and depict them accordingly. This approach can also be used with objects arrayed to depict parts' relationships to one another.

Appendices

Intrinsic Resources: As image-bearers, we possess qualities from birth that reflect some of God's attributes. While our developmental stage affects the manifestation of these qualities, they cannot be damaged or destroyed by experiences. Dr. Schwartz identified eight "C's" – curiosity, calm, compassion, connection, confidence, clarity, courage, and creativity – representing some of these important qualities. While this is not an exhaustive list, it helps to use it as a way to assess the degree to which we are able to lead our inner family in harmony with the Holy Spirit. The more of these qualities we notice, the more access we have to the resources needed for loving relationships.

Parts: Internal "family members" who have unique personalities with a range of thoughts, beliefs, emotions, experiences, and sensations. They exist from birth, but take on various roles as a result of experiences. Some of them are burdened by the roles they play, and others simply bring their unique and wonderful contribution to our functioning.

Protectors: When one member of the inner family experiences adversity, other members of the family take on jobs to protect the system from being overwhelmed by the impact of adversity. They are motivated by fear – fear that the distressing beliefs, emotions, images, and sensations will surface and flood the system. Some protectors, called "managers," *proactively* work to control our inner and outer worlds with a mission to never again allow the adversity to occur. Other protectors are "firefighters," first responders who *reactively* take action when something painful surfaces. All protectors have a positive intention.

Unblending: The process of differentiating the leader of the inner family from the various members of the family. Circumstances provoke parts, who rush forward with conflicting reactions. Acknowledging them, asking them to slow down or step back, and appreciating their positive intention creates a spacious environment for connection.

You-Turn: This term was coined by Dr. Schwartz to encourage focus on our inner world whenever we are provoked by something in the outer world. This is a change from the common practice of focusing on the other person and blaming them for distress. When we turn our attention inward and connect with the members of our inner family who are reacting to an external stimulus we can learn what they need. After attending to them, we are able to return our attention to the external relationship, drawing on our intrinsic resources and the presence of the Spirit to facilitate loving connection.

Acknowledgments

As soon as I was inspired to write this book, I realized I could not undertake the project alone. I reached out to three of my former Bethel classmates – pastors and fellow therapists – and Roxanne, Dan, and Taeler graciously agreed to be my first "advisors." Taeler's encouragement after reading the early draft of Part I helped me believe I could actually write a book, and reassured me that the content was useful. Monthly meetings with Dan to discuss theology were a highlight of the early months of the project. Roxanne was a steadfast source of support and input, reading almost every draft of every chapter of the book! Her encouragement sustained me.

I deeply appreciate Mark Strauss's guidance. At our first meeting he told me, "Yes, you have a book" and then gave me specific input that shaped the format. He read many drafts, giving me excellent suggestions and confidence in my hermeneutics.

Chris, a fellow "interpersonal neurobiology" and neuroscience nerd, sacrificed what little free time he has to carefully review Part II. I am indebted to him for his enthusiastic support for the project.

Susan Brown, LICSW, a nationally recognized expert on the impact of trauma on addiction, read Chapter 16 and said, "I wouldn't change a thing." As one of my early mentors, her support was a special source of encouragement.

After completing the draft manuscript, several "final" readers made the time to read and comment on the full manuscript. Dick Schwartz's willingness to read my manuscript is an example of his generosity and humility. In the many trainings, retreats, and consultation sessions I attended with him, he consistently met every individual in their circumstances with loving compassion, curiosity, and confidence that he could support their journey of healing. His example inspires my work with clients.

Miles McPherson is one of the busiest people I know, and I am filled with gratitude that he made the time to support this project. Graden brought a keen eye to the explanation of key IFS concepts, Linda reassured me that someone unfamiliar with the concepts would resonate with the material, and, as a fellow psychotherapist unfamiliar with IFS, Camden's interest in the model was encouraging. Mary Steege's book was the first to integrate Christian spirituality and IFS. It had a significant impact on my journey with the model, and her willingness to read and endorse the manuscript was a blessing.

I am also thankful for Brian Allain's tremendous resource – the Writing For Your Life website (*www.writingforyourlife.com*). A retired engineer, Brian is an unlikely champion of Christian writers. His accessibility and marketing expertise provided reassurance that I needed to undertake independent publishing. Through Brian, I met an indispensable source of support: my editor Adam Thomas.

Acknowledgments

Adam was the perfect partner for the editing process. As a pastor, writer, and highly reliable grammar nerd, he helped me fine-tune the manuscript so my perfectionistic parts could relax and trust that the final product would meet their approval. In our first meeting I said, "I'm a psychotherapist, not a writer." Adam said, "You're going to have to stop saying that." Okay, Adam, I'll say it, I'm also a writer! Adam also helped me design the cover and did the interior layout; each step of the process was both efficient and fun.

Above all, I acknowledge my courageous, tenacious clients whose commitment to their journey of healing motivates me and inspires me. They are my greatest teachers.

Finally, I'm grateful to my family for enthusiastically supporting me, not only with this project, but in every endeavor I have undertaken in response to the Spirit's inspiration.

Endnotes

Introduction
1. N.T. Wright, *God and the Pandemic: A Christian Reflection on the Coronavirus and its Aftermath*, 34.
2. R. Schwartz and M. Sweezy, *Internal Family Systems Therapy*, 2nd ed.
3. Ibid, 13
4. Ibid, 14
5. Ibid, 14
6. Ibid, 12
7. Ibid, 17

Chapter 1
8. For example, see Matthew 12:1-8, Luke 7:36-48, Luke 13:10-16
9. G. Boyd, *Repenting of Religion: Turning from Judgment to the Love of God*, 16.
10. Ibid, 16
11. P. Yancey, *Vanishing Grace*, 34

Chapter 2
12. G. Boyd, *Repenting of Religion: Turning from Judgment to the Love of God*, 6.
13. For example, 2 Corinthians 12:20, Galatians 5:19-21
14. G. Boyd, *Repenting of Religion: Turning from Judgment to the Love of God*, 6.

Chapter 3
15. R. Bell, *Love Wins* by 163-4
16. Ibid, 164
17. Ibid, 165-167

18 Ibid, 173 [italics mine]
19 *Christianity Today*, November 2017, 96
20 R. Bell, *Love Wins*, 113

Chapter 4
21 https://www.youtube.com/watch?v=Qs8Yjybs1Uk
22 D. Fosha, D.J. Siegel, & M.F. Solomon, *The Healing Power of Emotion*, vii.

Chapter 5
23 V.P. Hamilton, *The New International Commentary on the Old Testament: Genesis*, 181
24 D.L. Bock, *The NIV Application Commentary: Luke*, 83
25 Ibid, 128-29
26 Luke 6:6-11; Matthew 9:10-12, Matthew 23:1-39, and Luke 11:37-54
27 J.B. Green, *The New International Commentary on the New Testament: The Gospel of Luke*, 820.
28 R. Schwartz, *Introduction to the Internal Family Systems Model*, 9.
29 Ibid, 89
30 Ibid, 12
31 Ibid, 105, 114
32 For example, Luke 17:11-14, Mark 7:31-35, Matthew 9:1-2

Chapter 6
33 G. Maté, *In the Realm of Hungry Ghosts*.
34 D.J. Siegel, *The Developing Mind*, 2nd ed., 15.
35 B. van der Kolk, *The Body Keeps the Score*, 56-57.
36 Ibid and D.J. Siegel, *The Developing Mind*, 2nd ed., 17.
37 B. van der Kolk, *The Body Keeps the Score*, 56.
38 D.J. Siegel, *The Developing Mind*, 2nd ed., 18.
39 Ibid, 56
40 D.J. Siegel & M. Hartzell, *Parenting from the Inside Out*, 72.
41 D.J. Siegel, *The Developing Mind*, 2nd ed., 158; D.J. Siegel & M. Hartzell, *Parenting from the Inside Out*, 72.
42 B. van der Kolk, *The Body Keeps the Score*, 57.
43 Ibid, 61
44 S.W. Porges, *The Polyvagal Theory: Neurophysiological Foundations of Emotions, Attachment, Communication, and Self-regulation*.
45 D.J. Siegel & M. Hartzell, *Parenting from the Inside Out*, 72.
46 B. van der Kolk, *The Body Keeps the Score*, 57.
47 Ibid, 59

Endnotes

48 D.J. Siegel, *The Developing Mind, 2nd ed.*, 166.
49 B. van der Kolk, *The Body Keeps the Score*, 60.
50 Ibid, 62
51 D.J. Siegel, *The Developing Mind, 2nd ed.*, 47; D.J. Siegel & M. Hartzell, *Parenting from the Inside Out*, 11.
52 D.J. Siegel & M. Hartzell, *Parenting from the Inside Out*, 24.
53 Ibid, 25
54 D.J. Nakazawa, *The Angel and the Assassin*, 131.
55 Ibid, 11
56 D.J. Siegel, *The Developing Mind, 2nd ed.*, 52.
57 Ibid, 52
58 Ibid, 55
59 Ibid, 56
60 Ibid, 56
61 Ibid, 56
62 Ibid, 67
63 Ibid, 71
64 Ibid, 71
65 B. van der Kolk, *The Body Keeps the Score*, 176.

Chapter 7
66 Material in Chapter 7 is based on D.J. Siegel, *The Developing Mind, 2nd ed.*, 91-145.
67 Ibid, 121
68 Ibid, 92
69 Ibid, 100
70 Ibid, 100
71 Ibid, 141
72 B. van der Kolk, *The Body Keeps the Score*, 113.
73 Ibid, 129
74 Ibid, 110
75 D.J. Siegel, *The Developing Mind, 2nd ed.*, 112.
76 Ibid, 121-27; D.J. Siegel & M. Hartzell, *Parenting from the Inside Out*, 139-40.
77 D.J. Siegel, *The Developing Mind, 2nd ed.*, 130-31; D.J. Siegel & M. Hartzell, *Parenting from the Inside Out*, 141.
78 D.J. Siegel, *The Developing Mind, 2nd ed.*, 118-19.
79 B. van der Kolk, *The Body Keeps the Score*, 117.
80 D.J. Siegel, *The Developing Mind, 2nd ed.*, 134.
81 Ibid, 137

82 B. van der Kolk, *The Body Keeps the Score*, 120.
83 D.J. Siegel & M. Hartzell, *Parenting from the Inside Out*, 84, 87.
84 Ibid, 89

Chapter 8
85 D.J. Siegel & M. Hartzell, *Parenting from the Inside Out*, 53.
86 Ibid, 53
87 D.J. Siegel, *The Developing Mind*, 2nd ed., 149.
88 Ibid, 149
89 Ibid, 149
90 Ibid, 153
91 G. Maté, *When the Body Says No*, 200.
92 Ibid, 206
93 Ibid, 206-7
94 D.J. Siegel & M. Hartzell, *Parenting from the Inside Out*, 55.
95 G. Maté, *When the Body Says No*, 207.
96 Ibid, 216
97 Ibid, 115
98 A. Damasio, *Descartes' Error*, xvii.
99 Ibid, 53
100 Ibid, 159-60

Chapter 9
101 The study was done by Vincent Felitti and Robert Anda at Kaiser Permanente in San Diego. See https://www.cdc.gov/violenceprevention/childabuseneglect/acestudy/about.html for details.
102 B. van der Kolk, *The Body Keeps the Score*, 145.
103 D.J. Nakazawa, *Childhood Disrupted*, 25.
104 Ibid, 26
105 www.midss.org/sites/default/files/trauma.pdf
106 B. van der Kolk, *The Body Keeps the Score*, 53.
107 Ibid, 53, 80
108 Ibid, 62
109 Ibid, 63
110 Ibid, 67
111 Ibid, 127
112 Ibid, 128

Chapter 10
113 John 16:13, Romans 8:26, John 14:26

Endnotes

Chapter 11
114 R. Schwartz, *You Are the One You've Been Waiting For*

Chapter 12
115 R. Schwartz, *Introduction to the Internal Family Systems Model*, 90.
116 J.B. Green, *The New International Commentary on the New Testament: The Gospel of Luke*, 650.
117 Ibid, 651
118 For example, see Joshua 8:30-35
119 J.N. Oswalt, *The NIV Application Commentary: Isaiah*, 485.
120 Ibid, 486

Chapter 13
121 R. Schwartz, *Introduction to the Internal Family Systems Model*, 34.
122 P. Palmer, *Let Your Life Speak: Listening for the Voice of Vocation*

Chapter 14
123 R. Schwartz and M. Sweezy, *Internal Family Systems Therapy*, 2nd ed., 140.
124 J.H. Walton, *The NIV Application Commentary: Genesis*, 239.
125 Ibid, 238
126 Ibid, 232

Chapter 15
127 sarahbessey.com
128 M.R. McMinn, *Psychology, Theology, and Spirituality in Christian Counseling*, 214.
129 Ibid, 216

Chapter 16
130 G. Maté, *In the Realm of Hungry Ghosts*
131 Ibid
132 Ibid
133 Ibid
134 M. Lewis, *The Biology of Desire*, 177.
135 G. Maté, *In the Realm of Hungry Ghosts*
136 Ibid
137 J. Hari, *Chasing the Scream* pg. 171.
138 Ibid, 172

139 Ibid, 172
140 Ibid, 172
141 G. Maté, *In the Realm of Hungry Ghosts*
142 Ibid
143 Ibid; The author makes the distinction between drugs that have addictive potential and the assertion that drugs *directly cause* addiction.
144 Ibid
145 Ibid
146 C. Sykes in *Innovations and Elaborations in Internal Family Systems Therapy*, M. Sweezy & E.L. Ziskind, eds., 29.

Chapter 17
147 P. Yancey, *Disappointment with God*, 210.
148 Ibid, 217
149 Ibid, 251
150 N.T. Wright & M.F. Bird, *The New Testament in its World*, 491.
151 Ibid, 491
152 P. Yancey, *Disappointment with God*, 170/
153 Ibid, 140
154 M.L. Soards, *New International Biblical Commentary*, 205.
155 P. Yancey, *Disappointment with God*, 214.

Chapter 18
156 http://www.cac.org/transforming-our-pain-2016-07-03 [accessed 6/21/20]

Made in the USA
Columbia, SC
15 March 2024